COLLECTING POSTCARDS
In Colour
1914–1930

Collecting Postcards In Colour

1914–1930

BY VALERIE MONAHAN

BLANDFORD PRESS
Poole   Dorset

First published in the UK 1980

Copyright © Blandford Press Ltd,
Link House, West Street, Poole,
Dorset BH15 1LL

British Library Cataloguing in Publication Data

Monahan, Valerie
    Collecting postcards in colour, 1914–1930. –
    (Blandford colour series).
    1. Postal cards – Collectors and collecting
    I. Title
    769'.5   NC1872

ISBN 0 7137 1002 0 (Hardback edition)
ISBN 0 7137 1080 2 (Paperback edition)

Typeset by Butler & Tanner Ltd, Great Britain,
Printed in Hong Kong
by South China Printing Co.

Contents

Acknowledgements

Now is the time and here is the place for me to thank the many collectors and the postcard and newspaper publishers who have helped so much in the preparation of this book. I am especially grateful for the courtesy shown by the following publishers who have allowed me to reproduce examples of postcards and other material originally published by them: J. Bamforth & Co, Ltd, Holmfirth, Yorkshire; Mickey Mouse © Walt Disney Product-ions; J. Salmon Limited, Sevenoaks, Kent; The Daily Mail, Lon-don; The Daily Mirror, London; The Daily Telegraph, London; L. Tilley & Sons, Ledbury, Herefordshire; Raphael Tuck & Sons, Ltd, Blackpool, and Valentine & Sons, Ltd, Dundee.

My appreciation and thanks also to Mr Paul Babb, Mr A. James Butland, Mr Ron Griffiths, Mr Maurice Hewlett, Mrs Vivienne Kynaston, Mr Peter Lawrence, Mr Ken Lawson, Mr Brian Lund, Mr Ray Nash, Mr J. Howard Smith, Mr Frank Staff, Mr Tony Warr, and the Editors of the Postcard Mail, Mr Maurice Bray and Mr Colin Rhodes-Doughty.

Valerie Monahan
1980

In dedication to the memory
of A. James Butland

Introduction

Apart from the obvious hideousness of the First World War itself, the four years between 1914 and 1918 could very well be viewed by the postcard collecting population as the transitional years of their hobby. Up to the black summer of 1914, the postcard racks continued to be filled with a great variety of lavish enchantments; then, in step with everything and everyone else, postcards and their publishers went on war duty, and the racks were filled with patriotism and the kind of sentiment to suit the times.

The crunch came after the war, when postcard manufacturers were unable to resume their pre-war techniques of producing the elaborately decorated cards of bygone days. As it turned out they were obliged to reform their printing methods and to set their sights on new horizons – which was just as well, for in the new freedom-seeking climate of the 1920s there would have been no place for old themes, no matter how popular they had once been.

The post-war fever of the twenties gave rise to a determination to be done with the stifling restrictions of pre-war conventions. Women shortened their skirts, bobbed their hair, and decked themselves with spangles and bangles and lots of beads. Gleaming steel furniture, square-shaped crockery, cocktail cabinets and chromium plated lamps were all the rage. Bright Young Things discovered the Charleston and tapped their feet to the sound of Nick La Rocca and his Original Dixieland Jazz Band, and everyone whistled or hummed 'Bye-Bye' to the 'Blackbird'.

These were the days when conical shaped paper sweet bags

bulged with a couple of ounces of acid drops for a penny, and thick bars of Cadbury's Milk Chocolate could be bought for twopence. Days when petrol was cheap and motoring a pleasure (and salutes from the AA and RAC patrols to motorists displaying their badges were obligatory). The days of the crystal set, Lord John Sanger's Circus, Saturday night trips to the Music Hall and mid-week visits to the local 'flea-pit' to see the silent films.

They were also the days when the average wage of the working man was between ten shillings (now 50p) and fifteen shillings (75p) a week, and the idea of a fortune for the middle classes was to earn £20 a month. The dole queues lengthened; the kids from poor areas ran barefoot through the streets, many of them bow-legged with rickets caused by a constant lack of proper nutrition; the slum areas grew into forgotten hells, and the forgotten men steeped their anger in cheap beer while their women did menial labour to bolster the pittance of the dole pay.

Postcards – from whatever decade – rarely show pictures of the undramatic flotsam of human misery, and in line with that flippant phrase 'the poor are always with us' the black side of the poverty of the 1920s was swept under the postcard carpet. But whatever the sociologists, and others concerned with human behaviour, may say, the postcard publishers were right to concentrate their efforts on the fun and the pleasures and the reporting of affairs which were of general interest to their customers of the time.

Cards of the post-war years of the 1920s have now reached that certain age when they can be considered to be of collectable virtue; not surprisingly the ones to have mellowed most wonderfully are those which were highly desirable in the first place. And even though the days had gone when the postcard-buying public were spoiled for choice by all manner of extravagant enticements of pre-war production, there were still plenty of desirable cards around to catch the eye, many of which have survived to suit the requirements of present-day collectors. Promotional cards to further the cause of new commercial enterprise, cards to record the ebb and flow of social – and anti-social – events of the age, exciting cards to immortalise the achievements of the times, an endless supply of greetings and comic cards and views, and the riotously coloured cards of Art Deco design. The postcard racks were as full as ever they were, and among the millions of buyers were still the people who could not resist the pursuit of filling albums with a miscellany of the new modern postcards of the twenties. This fact makes quite extraordinary the view held in some quarters of the postcard world that by the 1920s the craze for collecting was over.

As it has turned out, the revival in the 1960s of the passion for collecting picture postcards has not only widened to include the nostalgic records of the twenties and succeeding decades, but also to contain the stuff of tomorrow's nostalgia to be seen in the current postcard racks.

This is a healthy prospect for the 1980s of a most absorbing hobby, for collectors themselves have decided that the matter of collecting postcards is a continuing process which dates from the time when they were first invented up to the present day, and beyond. And unlike the Victorian and Edwardian collectors, who merely pursued a delightfully relaxing pastime to be enjoyed by anyone and everyone, today's breed of devotees know beyond doubt the value of combining current pleasure with tomorrow's investment. Not for them the higgledy-piggledy order of earlier album arrangements; today's collections are preserved in recognizable compartments of categorical themes and chronological topography, often with careful documentation attached. From assemblages of this kind can be seen a continuous panorama of events and customs, and the differing artistic styles from the late nineteenth century through to the present day.

The signs of renewed interest in collecting up-to-date cards brings an air of stability to the hobby, giving established collectors even more scope to enhance their collections, while at the same time persuading newcomers to join in the fun, for there is nothing awesome or complicated about starting from square one – the modern card position. Square one was precisely the point at which the earliest collectors of picture postcards started, and now their cards of the pre-1920 period have followed in the footsteps of the more traditional objects of virtue, to take their place in the valuable world of antiques. Close on their heels are the postcard treasures of the twenties, and in due time the cards published from every other decade since the end of the First World War will follow. What wonderful opportunities are waiting in the wings for modern postcard publishers to grasp! And so this book, like its predecessor *Collecting Postcards, 1894–1914*, takes a nostalgic journey into the past by means of a commentary on cards that once were modern but have now grown old.

1 Boys in Khaki, Field Grey and Blue

By the beginning of the First World War the traffic in picture postcards had become a routine, as unexceptional as buying the daily bread. Postcard publishers were firmly established in a universally successful business which depended more upon the compulsive buying habits of the general public than upon the quirks and fads of the people who had a propensity for filling albums. Nevertheless, the fact that picture postcards were still eagerly collected twenty years after the novelty might reasonably have been expected to wane must have been of some significance, if not comfort, to those who produced them.

Twenty years of photographic reporting and reproducing in miniature the very best in talent and design had equipped postcard publishers well for their wartime function of providing a morale-boosting link between the men in the trenches and their families at home.

Not exactly the work that wins medals, nor even a mention in despatches, but throughout the duration of the First World War the army of publishers and printers, photographers and artists never flagged in their efforts to raise the spirits of the people. Picture postcards were produced which managed to articulate every emotion, every sentiment, every passing thought to flit through the minds of the millions of people who bought them. If there was one simple thing for which the public could be thankful in the dark days of that first Great War, it must surely have been the invention of picture postcards.

Among the first postcards with a wartime theme were those which related to the National Relief Fund, an appeal launched by the Prince of Wales on 7 August 1914 for the relief of distressed families. Most of the official postcards in support of this Fund featured photographs of the British Royal Family and famous military and naval leaders. C. W. Faulkner, however, reproduced a facsimile of the famous 'scrap of paper' – which was the term the German Chancellor, Bethmann Hollweg, had used contemptuously to dismiss the Treaty which was intended to preserve the neutrality of Belgium. The whole of the profit accrued from the sale of the Faulkner cards went to the National Relief Fund. Raphael Tuck and Sons Ltd donated an equally handsome contribution when they commissioned Harry Payne to design the famous 'Defenders of the Empire' postcard in aid of the Prince of Wales' Fund.

In November 1914 the Belgian Relief Fund was officially launched, and again postcards played their part. Cards 'issued under the Direction of Joseph Clarkson, Prestwick Park, near Manchester' were the authorized versions. They cost one penny each, and five shillings from every hundred cards sold went to this Fund. Very few hearts were left untouched by the pitiful plight of the Belgian people; purses and pockets were emptied of pennies for the postcards, and of shillings to send to the '*Daily Telegraph* Shilling Fund'.

Postcards played a significant role in the fund-raising efforts for the Red Cross. Early in 1914 the Kaiser ordered a special postal stationery card to be issued in support of the German Red Cross: this card portrays a uniformed Kaiser, his personal message and a facsimile of his signature. Another official postcard bears a brilliantly coloured picture of Austro-Hungarian troops marching into Czernowitz headed by a mounted officer of the Hussars. Switzerland published a great number of the Swiss Bundesfeier postal stationery cards. Designed by E. Burnand, these cards show a woman in a red dress bearing the Swiss emblem, sheltering a group of children beneath her cloak. On the reverse of the cards is a picture of Jean Henri Dunant, the founder of the Red Cross organization.

All the official postcards which were issued in aid of the Red Cross are now among those most coveted by collectors of First World War postcard history, but there were many other cards which told of their devotion to the Red Cross cause – postcards similar to the first shown in the illustrated section of this book, for example. This card, published by Tilley and Son, Ledbury, tells of the efforts of the Bosbury Red Cross Donkey, and on the reverse there is a printed record of money collected from towns and villages toured by the donkey. Donkeys were not the only four-legged friends to be recruited to the Red Cross drive for funds. Dogs of all breeds, shapes and sizes invaded towns and cities with collecting boxes strapped to their backs. These 'Collecting Jacks', as they were called, did a faithful job of hauling in the spare change, and there are many postcards still to be found showing this canine war effort which merit a worthy place in First World War collections.

As the war progressed, the medium of the picture postcard was used for many other appeals. Reproductions from some of R. Caton-Woodville's paintings of blind soldiers were sold in aid of St Dunstan's. There were postcards issued to help the British Ambulance Committee, the YMCA Hut Fund, the National Fund for Welsh Troops, the Lowland Regiments Badge Day to assist soldiers disabled and invalided at the Front, and the *Weekly Dispatch* Tobacco Fund Campaign. 'Smokes' for the troops was a cause dear to the heart of Bert Thomas, a caricaturist who worked for *Punch*. He designed the famous cartoon, ''Arf a Mo', Kaiser' and donated it to the *Weekly Dispatch* for their fund.

Across the Atlantic, the United States (although not directly involved in the war until 1917) were just as busy publishing cards to raise funds for worthy British and Allied causes. French war orphans were assisted by the New York 'Fatherless children of France' campaign, funded from the proceeds of special issues of Christmas cards. In London Lady Randolph Churchill, Mrs Hoover, and Senator Chauncey Depew were among the founders of the American Women's War Fund, and postcards were used in their fund-raising campaign.

Later in the war, subscribing to the 'National War Bond Tanks' fund became a drain on pockets and purses. There were several photographic cards published showing tanks which were stationed at strategic points in London and British provincial cities, where the public were invited to donate sums to the War Bond Campaign. A. M. Davis and Co. also published a complete set of twelve coloured battle drawings which were inscribed on the reverse side as War Bond Campaign postcards. There were similar schemes in France, Italy and Germany to raise War Loans by the sale of postcards of suitably patriotic design.

The rattle of collecting boxes for worthy causes inspired many people to break into verse, and a number of dreadfully emotional odes are to be found on relief cards. 'The Soldier's Cigarette' by Sep. Douthwaite is one of the better poetic efforts. Douthwaite also gave lyrical support to the Purple Cross Service, who published a postcard of his appeal for horses. Then there is a long series of postcards issued by the National Federation of Discharged and Demobilized Sailors and Soldiers, and one of the first to appear showing the British Cavalry on the Somme has on its reverse side a poem reprinted from the *Hackney Spectator* with the note that 'The proceeds of the Sale of this poem goes towards the Fund'.

Most of these relief-fund or charity appeal cards are in good supply today, and for collectors who are attempting to build up a chronological account of the First World War period there is an excellent variety from which to choose.

Patriotic cards of all nations

National flags and national emblems had decorated many a postcard long before the summer of 1914, but then they were used more as symbols of identity than as a show of national pride. The advent of the First World War brought a fresh and stronger meaning to the cause of patriotism. In a riot of colour, the flags of all nations involved in the war waved their defiance across billions of postcards.

The British Bulldog was symbolized as the menace from whom the impudent German Dachshund would flee in terror. German cartoonists saw the British Tommy as a football-crazy yokel –

his favourite sport making him fleet of foot when running away from German shells; French soldiers were described as fashionable fops exquisitely uniformed by the *haute couture*; Russians were invariably shown as red-nosed layabouts, lying tipsy among the vodka bottles. Italian caricaturists saw the German soldiers as darkly satanic beasts who traded in wholesale murder, and the Italian card which portrays a Belgian street cobbled with the skulls of slain villagers must have been assured first place in the nightmare stakes.

From British postcard publishers came an endless choice of patriotic morale-boosters, one of the most skilful of which was drawn by William Armitage and published by Boot's Cash Chemists Ltd. Under the title 'A Tribute to our Colonies', this card depicts the head of the British Lion, with the names New Zealand, Australia, Canada, the African Colonies and India woven into its mane – below which is the caption 'The Glory of a Lion is his Mane' (Figure 1).

With or without flags, sepia and coloured photographs and portraits of all the national war leaders were certain favourites with the postcard-buying public. In Britain, Birn Brothers issued an attractive series (see plates nos 65 and 66) which honoured all

Figure 1. 'A Tribute to our Colonies'

ranks. Another colourful series was entitled 'Men of the Moment', with oval sepia photographs of wartime heroes like Lord Kitchener, Admiral Jellicoe and Sir John French, surrounded by the bold red, white and blue of the Union Jack; and under the heading 'The European War, 1914' Raphael Tuck and Sons Ltd produced a long series of 'Notabilities' in dignified sepia (Figure 2). Then there were a large number of sepia-tinted French postcards of General Joffre, Marshal Foch, General Petain, King Albert of the Belgians and many other French and Belgian leaders, and a galaxy of attractive sets with an *Entente Cordiale* theme. Photographs of President Wilson, President Poincaré, Kaiser Wilhelm, King George V, Queen Mary, and the Prince of Wales were also chosen to spearhead the drive for national loyalties and patriotism.

Figure 2. Admiral Sir Hedworth Meux

The Philco Publishing Co. and Millar and Lang's 'National Series' produced many of the 'Hands Across the Sea' themes of crossed flags flanking clasped hands, surrounded or supported by vignettes of speeding trains, ships and aeroplanes, which formed an immensely colourful expression of the sentiment of the times. Inter-Art published a great number of their 'Patriotic' series of postcards, some with emotive blood-rousing captions like, 'We don't want to fight – but by JINGO if we do....', intended no doubt to persuade the most timid that they too had chests to expand with pride – given the opportunity!

In September 1914 Jarrold and Sons Ltd of Norwich published postcards of the '*Punch* War Cartoons'. These were black line-drawings against a pale yellow background. Caricatures lampooning the Kaiser, drawn by Bernard Partridge and L. Raven-Hill, were the main attractions of this series. Sold in packets of twelve cards for one shilling, the cartoons rank among the first of a long line of anti-German propaganda postcards to be published in Britain.

Postcard publishers in Germany were no less fervent in their efforts to perk up the spirits of their own countrymen, and, while Germany may have lost the war, in one field at least she never yielded her claim to supremacy: she continued to produce picture postcards of the highest quality. True, the subject matter of many of the wartime postcards was repugnant to her enemies, but nations at war are not expected to be pleasant to each other, and while some of the German propaganda cartoons were odiously explicit in their hatred of nations allied against her, those same Allies were by no means averse to producing quite a few blood-curdling examples of their own to signify their abomination of Germany.

The days of the First World War are now long past, and since then the world has seen far greater evils in the dictates of Corporal Hitler, so that the sins of the Kaiser have been transformed into virtues by comparison. In fact King Edward VII's nephew, Kaiser Wilhelm II, has now become a twentieth-century folk hero to collectors of militaria, and First World War postcards from Germany are in great demand by collectors. Thanks to Michael

Clarke of 'Desiderata' in West Germany, today's collectors have been given the rare chance of adding some superb First World War material to their collections: brilliantly coloured drawings of Allied leaders designed by the famous cartoonist Trier, who later fled to Britain from Eastern Europe for refuge; gorgeous postcards signed by Brynolf Wennerberg, who was known more for his renderings of Edwardian beauties dressed for the beach than for his wartime sketches of pretty German Frauleins being courted by élitist German officers; cheeky cartoons like the one of Sir Edward Grey depicted as an evil cup over which an old crone is stirring 'the latest brew of British wickedness' (Sir Edward was always portrayed as the arch villain); plaintive cartoons expressing German displeasure at the refusal of the American President Wilson to help Germany – 'Uncle Sam', they declared, 'is flat on his back'.

Then there were the German cards designed by leading poster artists of the day, Carl Diehl, P. O. Engelhardt and B. Dondorf – to mention a few who helped to create the postcards for an extensive series entitled 'Children in Uniform'. A series of laughing children, jeering children, tiny tots with angelic faces beneath spiked helmets goading Allied soldiers to their deaths at the point of fixed bayonets. Questionable taste? No less questionable were some of the postcards drawn by British and French artists which featured children, and war is a tasteless game in any language.

Postcards of the Kaiser and his family were presented in glowing style by such artists as Renatus, Ehrlich and Voigt. Beautifully designed and coloured symbolic cards came from Franz Stassen – postcards like the one entitled 'Zur Walstatt', a painting of an officer with naked sword leading his men into action beneath a pair of female warriors mounted on white horses, and another by Stassen which shows an armoured and winged Germania withdrawing a flaming sword from its scabbard, with Infantry, Cavalry and Zeppelin in the background.

By 1917 the patriotic postcard scene was further enhanced by the sight of the 'Stars and Stripes' when the United States joined forces with the European Allies. There were gloriously coloured examples of 'Old Glory' covering the whole of the picture side of

American-produced cards; enchanting additions to the patriotic pageant of glamour postcards, drawn by traditional French artists such as Xavier Sager, in the form of lovely girls dressed in red, white and blue creations with accentuated stars and striped designs; plentifully published postcards of Uncle Sam and John Bull against backgrounds of Allied flags that would not furl.

There is little doubt that patriotism on a postcard gladdens the eye and lends brightness to the pages of the postcard album.

The realism of battle postcards

Though postcard publishers were well practised in the art of 'on the spot' photography, whatever the event, they were not officially allowed to use their expertise during the war years due to the imposition of strictly observed censorship laws. Photographers were nonetheless commissioned by postcard publishers to carry their cameras to the Front line, and some of these cameramen contrived to take some excellent pictures which their publishers managed to print and publish in neutral countries. Most of the cards depicting early battle scenes, however, were artist-drawn, and were very often published in sets of six or more cards. Then in 1916 the Press Bureau gave the *Daily Mail* the sole right to reproduce on postcards the pictures of Western Front battles taken by their official photographers – on condition that half the profits from the sale of the cards was given to army relief funds. The *Daily Mail* Battle Pictures of 'Official War Photographs', each card bearing the imprint 'Passed by Censor' in the top left-hand corner of the address side, were an immediate success – hardly surprising, when so many of the cards, like the one illustrated in Figure 3, showed the face of someone's father, husband, or son. British families throughout the land could not get their fill, the clamour for these cards was so great. By October 1916 the *Daily Mail* was manufacturing albums, to contain 240 of their Battle Pictures, which could be purchased from newsagents for 2s 6d (now 12½p), and these too went like hot cakes. The cards themselves were sold in series of eight for sixpence (2½p), and while most were printed in sepia some of the sets were in colour.

There were a number of other interesting series issued by

Figure 3. Northumberland Fusiliers

French, German and Italian publishers to show the more non-combatant aspects of life at the Front, as there were in Britain. One of the most successful British series in this category was issued by the Photochrom Co. Ltd of London and Tunbridge Wells, entitled 'On Active Service by Air, Land and Sea'. A good example from this series is shown in Plate 16.

At a more personal level, front-line soldiers were not to be thwarted from sending the occasional picture postcard of themselves to their families at home. While they were always mindful of the censorship restrictions they managed to find local photographers to snap them in small friendly groups against anonymous, non-committal backgrounds. These photographs were then transformed into postcards and sent home franked by the Field Post Offices. Such cards now play a role in records of First World War history.

Keeping the home fires burning

While the men were away fighting for honour and freedom, the women rolled up their sleeves and did the work of men at home, and did it marvellously. The unusual sight of women humping coal, collecting the mail, 'screwing down' the yeast at the breweries, driving trams, steamrollers and mail vans, was not the sort of stuff in which the regular postcard publishers were interested – although they did take notice of the women at work in the ammunition factories.

It is thanks to the private photographers and the small local printers that present-day collectors are able to add these gems of First World War social history to their collections. There are not too many of these real photographic cards about, for local printers were chary of publishing long runs of any one subject, but it is possible to find postcards of fascinating detail which record wartime lassies shouldering the jobs of men (see Figure 4). Women railway porters, barbers, window cleaners (see Plate 6), gas workers, lumberjacks, cobblers and farriers could be seen, even women tar sprayers renewing the surface of Regent

Figure 4. Women war workers

23

Street, London. Most of these then extraordinary female activities were chronicled on postcards and sold in the local newspaper shops.

In praise of nurses

Members of the nursing profession seldom make the headlines for the work they do, and Nurse Edith Cavell was no exception until the day she was caught in Belgium helping English and French soldiers to escape over the Dutch frontier. With Philippe Bauqu, her associate in the escape plans, Nurse Cavell was arrested, court-martialled, condemned to death and shot; and the name Nurse Edith Cavell was blazoned across the world.

There are many postcards, some of which were issued in sets, to tell the heroic story of Nurse Cavell. The most famous picture of her is one showing her with her dogs, and the most popular version to be published was silk printed on a plain-backed card. This calmly serene picture was also used in 1916 on a postcard in aid of the Belgian Soldiers Fund (Plate 2).

The death by shooting of this most courageous of women prompted the *Daily Mirror* to establish the Nurse Cavell Memorial Fund to 'perpetuate the memory of one of England's noblest Englishwomen by the establishment of an Edith Cavell Home for Nurses'. A special charity matinee on behalf of the fund was held at the London Hippodrome on 15 November 1915. Among the artists who prepared the special art souvenir programme were many well known to postcard collectors, including John Hassell, Lawson Wood, Hilda Cowham, Will Owen and W. Barribal.

Postcards featuring nurses were again brought into sharp focus when British postcard collector, Mrs Sylvia Haynes, staged an exhibition of her nursing postcards at the Islington Museum in aid of the Elizabeth Garrett Anderson Hospital – the hospital which is staffed solely by women for women. It was an imaginative and heart-warming exercise to show the postcard tributes which have been paid to the nursing profession over the years.

It's a Long, Long Way to Tipperary!

There was nothing new about song cards; from early in postcard history they had been among the best-selling themes. Davidson Brothers had commissioned artists like Tom Browne, Will Owen and Dudley Hardy to interpret chosen song titles for their 'Illustrated Songs' series. Raphael Tuck and Sons, Valentine and Sons, Millar and Lang, and Shamrock and Co. had also burst into song on postcards. But whenever song cards are mentioned the name Bamforth and Co. springs to mind before all other postcard publishers.

James Bamforth, of Holmfirth in Yorkshire, was a keen photographer with an interest in early cinematography. Using his family and friends posing as models against a variety of backgrounds he produced lantern slides to entertain the public. By the beginning of the new century, when it was seen that the newfangled postcard had come to stay, James Bamforth and his sons saw an exciting prospect within the postcard market for another outlet for their collection of lantern slides. From their vast store of photographs and slides they started to produce sets of glossy monochrome cards, adapting them to suit the titles of well-loved songs and hymns. It was not long before the business of James Bamforth had expanded into producing coloured versions of songs like 'Don't Go down the Mine, Dad', and hymns such as 'Abide with me'. A strict numbering system was applied to the new coloured types of song cards, which started at No 4,500, and according to the check-list compiled by Major Robert Scherer of Florida, USA there were some six hundred and twenty nine sets published up to and during the First World War. During the war Bamforth song cards were firm favourites with the postcard-buying public – especially when new songs were added to the Bamforth repertoire. One of these songs was written and composed by Jack Judge and Harry Williams and was first heard in the music halls only two years before war broke out. It was a song which was to echo through the length and breadth of Europe before the war was finished: a rousing little ditty which prompted the Frenchwomen to rename the Scottish bonnets they wore as a tribute to the Highlanders 'Tipperary Hats' – after the 'soldiers' song', 'It's a Long, Long Way to Tipperary'.

'Tipperary' was also included among the song titles of the sets

25

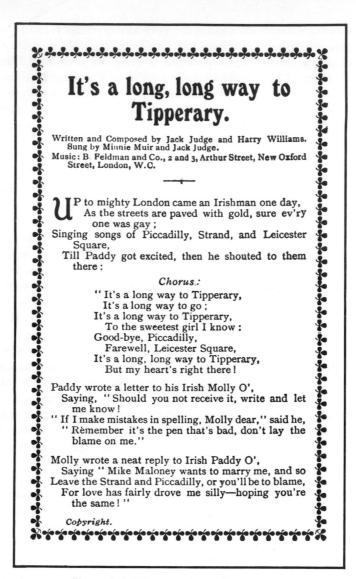

It's a long, long way to Tipperary.

Written and Composed by Jack Judge and Harry Williams.
Sung by Minnie Muir and Jack Judge.
Music: B. Feldman and Co., 2 and 3, Arthur Street, New Oxford Street, London, W.C.

UP to mighty London came an Irishman one day,
   As the streets are paved with gold, sure ev'ry
      one was gay ;
Singing songs of Piccadilly, Strand, and Leicester
      Square,
   Till Paddy got excited, then he shouted to them
      there :

Chorus:
   "It's a long way to Tipperary,
   It's a long way to go ;
   It's a long way to Tipperary,
      To the sweetest girl I know :
   Good-bye, Piccadilly,
      Farewell, Leicester Square,
   It's a long, long way to Tipperary,
      But my heart's right there !

Paddy wrote a letter to his Irish Molly O',
   Saying, "Should you not receive it, write and let
      me know !
" If I make mistakes in spelling, Molly dear," said he,
   " Remember it's the pen that's bad, don't lay the
      blame on me."

Molly wrote a neat reply to Irish Paddy O',
   Saying " Mike Maloney wants to marry me, and so
Leave the Strand and Piccadilly, or you'll be to blame,
   For love has fairly drove me silly—hoping you're
      the same ! "

Copyright.

Figure 5. A 'Correspondence (Song) Card'

of 'Correspondence (Song) cards' published by F.McG. Ltd, of London. These cards were sold in packets of six for one penny, and each packet bore the legend 'Send these to your SAILOR & SOLDIER FRIENDS. They will be appreciated.' At six for a penny Mr F. McG. made his contribution, even though his cards, like the one in Figure 5, were merely pictureless verses printed on thin card with 'Correspondence (Song) Card' inscribed on the back in place of the usual 'POST CARD'.

The songs of the past were heavily laced with the sort of smothering sentiment which people today tend to find highly unpalatable, but in those days it was all sincerely meant, as fragrant as the 'Roses of Picardy' – and just as haunting

The humour of the First World War

Some of the people most admired are those who can cheer up the rest with a good belly laugh when life is at its unfunniest. And The First World War was certainly one of the unfunniest events ever to take place in the records of human history. But there were clowns, jesters and cartoonists to lighten the darkness. Cartoonists of all the contending nations were the cheer leaders of that war. Dedicated to their task of injecting a spot of humour or satire into the gloomiest situations, they gave a marathon performance of producing a dazzling parade of picture postcard 'tonics' for the people throughout the war. The typically laconic British humour was well to the fore in the First World War comic field, with millions of cards to raise a smile being churned out by the large and small postcard publishers. Postcard racks were full of the work of Donald McGill, Lawson Wood, Fred Spurgin, George Studdy, Reg Carter, G. F. Christie, Hilda Cowham, D. Tempest, G. M. Payne, Ludgate, Reg Maurice, T. Gilson and G. E. Shepheard – to mention just a few of the well-known signatures to be found on comic postcards during that period.

Lampooning the Kaiser was obviously a favourite pastime, and among the best – and the most valuable – of these 'let's have a go at the Kaiser' cards were Louis Wain's Kaiser cat drawings, and the sparkling sketches drawn by Sancha and entitled 'Aesop's Fables, up to date'. Apart from the satirical drawings depicting

I vouldn't leave mine leedle rabbit hole vor you.

Figure 6. A Bamforth 'War Cartoon'

the Kaiser as a mail-fisted monster with moustaches of Mephistophelian proportions (see Figure 6), there was work for the writers of captions and verse, who had researched well the short-comings of Wilhelm II and were happily employed. Armed with the fact that the Kaiser was well known for being on very 'personal terms with the Deity', they placed exquisite emphasis upon the theme *'Mein Gott und mir'*, and predictably enough many of the pithy postcard titles and poems reflected the wonder of the Allies about the God to whom the Kaiser referred, since their God could only be on the side of right, and the Kaiser was quite patently on the other (Figure 7).

But amid the riot of brilliantly coloured gaiety of First World War comic postcards emerged a series in sepia which was to become a classic of the times. The creation of 'Old Bill' by Captain Bruce Bairnsfather for his 'Fragments from France' series was a

THE KAISER'S DREAM.

THERE'S a story now current, though strange it
    may seem,
      Of the great Kaiser Bill and a wonderful dream.
      Being tired of the Allies, he lay down in bed,
And, amongst other things he dreamt he was dead.
On leaving the earth to Heaven, he went straight,
Arriving up there, he knocked at the gate,
But St. Peter looked out, and in voice loud and clear,
Said " Begone Kaiser Bill, we don't want you here."
Well, says the Kaiser, that's very uncivil,
I suppose after that, I must go to the Devil ?
So he turned on his heel, and off he did go
At the top of his speed to the regions below,
And when he got there he was filled with dismay,
For, while waiting outside, he heard Old Nick say
To his imps : " Now look here, boys, I give you all warning,
I'm expecting the Kaiser down here in the morning ;
But don't let him in, for to me its quite clear,
He's a very bad man, and we don't want him here.
If he ever gets in we'll have no end of quarrels,
In fact, I'm afraid he'll corrupt our good morals."
" Oh, Satan, my dear friend," the Kaiser then cried,
"Excuse me for listening while waiting outside ;
If you don't admit me, then where can I go,
Oh do let me in, for I'm feeling quite cold.
And if you want money, I've plenty of gold ;
Let me sit in a corner, no matter how hot ; "
" No, no," said Old Nickie, "most certainly not ;
We do not admit folks for riches or wealth ;
Here are sulphur and matches, make a Hell for yourself."
Then he kicked William out, and vanished in smoke,
And just at that moment the Kaiser awoke.
He jumped out of bed in a shivering sweat ;
And said " Well. that dream I'll never forget :
That I won't go to Heaven I know very well,
But it 's really too bad to be kicked out of Hell."

Figure 7. An anti-Kaiser postcard

composite tribute to the endurance and humour of the British
Tommy, drawn not from imagination but from the mud and
slush of the trenches among the men the artist admired so much.

Figure 8. 'The Nest'

The *Bystander* published six different editions of the Bairnsfather sketches – at one shilling (now 5p) a copy for the standard print, and five shillings and sixpence ($27\frac{1}{2}$p) for the *de luxe* impressions. From these 'Fragments from France' drawings nine sets of six postcards were reproduced and published. A typical example of the perceptive warmth of Bruce Bairnsfather's humour is seen in Figure 8, an illustration of a postcard from Series 8.

A spot of First World War sauce!

Drawings of pretty girls with sultry eyes and provocative poses, wearing only the barest of essentials, were exactly the right sort of sauce to spice up the rations of bully-beef and biscuits, and an élite regiment of French artists saw to it that the troops were well nourished.

Postcard fantasias of dreamily delectable femininity may have been unlikely substitutes for many of the wives and sweethearts back home, but every man could dream, and in the dreaming exorcise the nightmare of the realities of war. For this reason alone, if ever there had been a 'Croix de Guerre' invented for the war service of 'drawing glamour', then names like Raphael Kirchner, Leo Fontan, Maurice Millière, A. Penot, Suzanne Meunier, Herouard, L. Peltier, Maurice Pepin, Ouillon ꞌCarreré A. Jarach, Xavier Sager, F. Fabiano, Jean Tam, René Vincent, A. Mauzan, Maggy Monier, G. Nanni, Federico Ribas, A. Terzi, A. Torello and G. Leonnec would have topped the list of those deserving honours.

Nowadays the sight of the delicious naughtiness of this wartime glamour – or saucy pin-up postcards – appears a trifle tame compared with the more explicit examples of post-war eras, but for the four years between 1914 and 1918, when men saw only the colours of mud and slime and blood, and their nostrils took for granted the disagreeable scents of the trenches, the tantalizing visions of pastel-coloured drawings of intriguing mademoiselles (perhaps from Armentières!), reproduced on pieces of pasteboard, was enough to reassure even the most prosaic of soldiers that, one day, the nightmares must end, and they would awake to find themselves homeward bound to the less ethereal, but much more substantial and satisfying, hearths of love.

The Victoria Cross, for outstanding courage
Real photographs, black and white portraits, and action pictures in full colour were all published on postcards to commemorate the sort of courage to earn a VC. J. C. Beagles and Co. Ltd, Faulkner and Co. Ltd and the Rotary Photographic Co. were well to the front of postcard publishers ready with their cameras to record and honour the mettle of the most valiant. Men like the Scotsman, No 91608, Corporal J. L. Dawson of the 187th Co. Royal Engineers, who found three leaking gas cylinders close to a trench full of his men under a gas attack at the Hohenzollern Redoubt. Under heavy fire he rolled the cylinders away from the trench and fired rifle bullets into them to allow the gas to

gave during the First World War. 'Here are the rolls of muslin, here are the bobbins of silks, and here are the designs – get on with it!' was probably the terse command to the French embroideresses bent upon doing their bit for the war. No wonder that by the time some of them were nearing the end of the umpteenth version of the same design stitches were apt to wander from the lines of the original pattern, and spelling errors were made in the text. What weariness must have been borne by the women who threaded their silks through the million or so metres of muslin required to produce the many thousands of different floral designs of sentimental greeting. Yet the intricacies of translating in silk the patterns for regimental crests and badges, and some of the more complex ideas of patriotism, must have been even more demanding, since the precise detail of such designs was of paramount importance to the regiments and nations concerned.

The huge variety of embroidered silk postcards which were produced in the First World War would fill an average-sized album several times over. There were roses and pansies and violets and forget-me-nots, clustered in baskets and wheelbarrows, in garlands and sprays and geometrically arranged bouquets, to wish the world and its relations a 'Happy Birthday' morning; there was holly and mistletoe and delicate trails of ivy decorating central themes of churches and cottages to accompany conventional Christmas greetings; and for Easter the rabbits and lambs were to be seen gambolling in silk amid the crocuses and daffodils. Then there were the bold, brave colours of patriotism, and the crests of regimental pride.

Sometimes the designs were imposed upon one flat piece of muslin, and sometimes on two pieces to form an envelope shape into which a separate greetings card or small silk handkerchief could be inserted – and sometimes, much to the satisfaction of today's collectors, those small separate greetings cards are found to have been designed and signed by Xavier Sager, who was better known for his daring drawings of pretty ladies.

To help these beautiful embroidered silk postcards to withstand the rigours of being sent through the post, each card was placed in specially made sepia pellucid envelopes, which were useful for keeping the cards in pristine condition but not for addressing, as one would an ordinary envelope. But, however they arrived at their destinations, embroidered silk postcards with their personal messages – 'To Mother', 'To my dear Sister', 'Sweetheart', 'My dear Friend', etc. – were greatly treasured, and usually carefully preserved, by the relatives and friends of the troops who sent them.

Woven Silk 'Flames' postcards

The number of woven silk postcards produced during the First World War are now hard and very expensive to find, especially those which bore woven portraits of notable people of the times, such as President Wilson, Lloyd-George, Nurse Cavell and international war leaders.

Until the mid-1970s, however, it was still possible to find a fair choice of a series of cards which are popularly known as the 'Flames' silks. Manufactured and distributed by Neyret Frères of France, these cards show the blazing vividness of towns and buildings being consumed by fire.

There are over sixty different examples of 'Flames' known to collectors, but while it was possible in 1974–75 to purchase these cards for one or two pounds, regardless of any particular rarity attached to the specimens, the story is rather different now, for prices have soared well into double figures even for the most commonplace types.

The tragedy of war

Cards showing a heap of ruins caused by the devastation of war are usually looked upon – or down on – as the poor relations of postcard-collecting categories. Booklets of perforated postcards depicting war damage to the towns and villages of Belgium and France were printed and dispensed with monotonous regularity – memorials in sepia to the suffering and waste caused by the desecration of war.

No one seems to know why so many of these cards were produced, for the sight of a collection of them in an album does nothing to raise the spirits (nor do they prick the consciences of people today, who have become numbed, if not immune, to the sight of instant violence and death and evil destruction at the touch of a television switch). Yet sometimes, by a trick of the imagination, and a closer look at some of the pictures of those broken villages of Belgium and France, a different view can be conjured. A little village, the sun slanting on the tiled rooftops of houses painted white; children playing in the cobbled street; an old woman nodding to her dreams in an open doorway; the belfry tower and the remembered sound of the carillon chime. Then the sepia monstrosity of houses turned to rubble, no children playing, no old women browsing in the sun, and only a black hole in the church tower where the clock should have been. Homes gone, hardship and a desolate future facing whoever may have survived, and the silence of the bells.

Perhaps this fantasy of one of so many shattered villages is not too strange a reason why so many war damage postcards were produced, for of all the millions of First World War cards these tell the truth of the waste and the cruelty and the absolute futility of war.

2   *A Decade of Social History on Postcards*

City highways, civic buildings, churches and cathedrals, castles and country houses, crowded beaches and country pastures – all can be seen in splendid abundance on postcards, from the time when they were first invented right up to the present day. Publishing business-like views was, and still is, the staple recipe for success of all the established manufacturers of postcards. All the same, these commonplace cards play a necessary part in building up records of social history in modern postcard collections. For this reason alone they should not be dismissed as being of little value, but recognized as the bare branches of a tree upon which can be added the scarcer delights of animated nostalgia which every devotee of social history seeks.

Decade by decade, since 1894 when the sending and receiving of postcards first flaunted its appeal, the kaleidoscope of events of the times has faithfully been recorded on postcards, and the bells which pealed to ring in the decade of the 1920s promised no less activity on the postcard producing front.

1920

Dominated by 'Peace at Last' themes, 1920 was the year which saw the birth of the League of Nations, and there were postcards to record the facsimiles of the signatures to the Versailles Treaty (oddly reminiscent of what some may remember as another 'Scrap of Paper'). On Armistice Day, 11 November 1920, King George V unveiled the Cenotaph in Whitehall, London, and at

11 o'clock on the morning of that appointed day Britons throughout the land bowed their heads in silent remembrance. The Cenotaph – the monument designed by Sir Edwin Lutyens to preserve the memory of men of all creeds who had died in the war – has now become a familiar London landmark, to be featured on postcards along with Nelson's Column, the Houses of Parliament and Buckingham Palace. The photographic cards which were snapped in the split second after the two minutes of national silence captured more clearly the depth of a nation's homage, and its grief.

On the same day a British soldier was buried in Westminster Abbey. There were several sets of postcards to describe this event in neat formal sepia, but none disclose the poignant story of how this soldier was to be chosen as the Everyman of the fallen, henceforth named the Unknown Warrior. How the coffins bearing the bodies of six anonymous men who were killed in action were brought to a hut near Arras, where an officer with eyes closed was waiting to rest his hand on one of the six, was a moment not to be shared with the cameras. But the sets of cards show views of HMS *Verdun* leaving Boulogne with the body of the Unknown Warrior aboard, and the flag-shrouded coffin later being lifted on to the waiting gun-carriage in the presence of the King and Queen and Lord Haig, and there are a number of cards to be found to describe official wreaths, including one from the King with the inscription 'In proud memory of those Warriors who died unknown in the Great War'.

1920 was the year which saw the first automatic petrol feed pump being installed in London, and cards are to be found showing this new elongated contraption filling the tanks of taxis and motor cars while their drivers looked on in wonder. It was also another vintage year for women, when Oxford University conferred degrees upon fifty of their women graduates, an idea sufficiently novel to attract the interest of postcard publishers, prompting a spate of photographs of these exalted women in their caps and gowns. New female students were quickly termed 'undergraduettes' by the Press, a term which was seized upon by cartoonists and writers of postcard captions – much to the chagrin of the ladies themselves who repeatedly let it be known that their proper address was 'woman undergraduate'.

In 1904 Thomas Farrow opened a bank in Cheapside, London for small depositors, who were invited to open accounts with as little as one pound. By the outbreak of the 1914–18 war, Farrow's Bank had seventy-five branches to its credit, and extensive advertising in all the national newspapers continued to attract large numbers of the 'poor people' for whom it had been founded right up to December 1920, when it crashed. There were many photographs to record the crowds clamouring for the return of their hard-earned savings – and some of these found their way onto postcards – but these small depositors lost everything, and Thomas Farrow was charged with fraud and sent to jail for four years.

1921

The day when Charlie Chaplin returned to London from Hollywood after ten years of achieving fame as the comic in a little bowler, big boots and with a funny walk, twirling a walking stick, was a red-letter occasion for thousands of his cheering fans. The crowds were out in force to meet him at Waterloo Station, and they blocked Piccadilly for hours after he had arrived at the Ritz Hotel. Charlie may have been away from his homeland for a long time, but his fans had been kept well informed by the picture postcards of his successes in America, and they knew that his heart was in the right place because the proceeds from some of those cards went to the benefit of Charlie's pet charities. One such postcard, entitled 'Charlie Chaplin in the Post Office', was sold to help the Post Office Orphans Homes at Christmas 1915, which showed a perceptive concern for charities which were not engaged in wartime fund-raising. Plain-backed 'Red Letter' cards were published by Essanay, the firm with the Red Indian trademark, of Charlie in a variety of play-pictorial situations, and all of them are eagerly collected today (see Figure 9).

Late in the afternoon of 24 August 1921, tragedy struck when the R38 – the airship built for the United States Navy – flew over Hull and exploded while attempting to turn over the Humber.

(Charlie Chaplin.)   A Small Flirtation.   (Charlie's Night Out.)

Figure 9. A typical Chaplin pose

There were forty-nine British and American officers aboard the R38 during this last test flight, and only five of them survived. There are postcards of the airship before the disaster, and several of the mangled structure floating in the sea after the crash.

This was the year in which Chequers, the country home of Lord and Lady Lee of Fareham, was added to the long list of stately homes which were photographed for postcards. These were produced to mark the presentation of Chequers by Lord and Lady Lee to the State for the personal use of Prime Ministers. Mr Lloyd-George was the first occupant.

In the United States Jack Dempsey, the American boxer, defended his title of heavyweight champion of the world by knocking out Frenchman Georges Carpentier in front of ninety thousand people at Jersey City on 2 July 1921. Particular attention was paid to this exciting event by both American and British postcard publishers. Australia won the first three cricket Test Matches, and the Ashes for that year, and to conform with the long-standing custom there were plenty of cards to portray the winning team. And Steve Donoghue – always a favourite subject for postcards with a horse-racing theme – was up on Humorist to win the 1921 Derby by a neck from Craig-an-Eran.

In September 1921 Sir Ernest Shackleton set sail in *The Quest* on what was to be his last journey to the Antarctic. The postcards issued to bid him farewell, showing Shackleton and his crew on board his ship, were followed a few months later by his 'In Memoriam' cards. He died in South Georgia on 5 January 1922.

1922

This was the year when postcard publishers, both large and small, were at their busiest, a phenomenon which always seemed to occur when there was some Royal occasion to commemorate. In 1922 there was a Royal marriage – between Princess Mary, the Princess Royal, and Viscount Lascelles – and postcards galore were available to fill the albums of loyal subjects. In Germany there was another wedding, but the glare of publicity surrounding the marriage of ex-Kaiser Wilhelm to Princess Hermine von Schonaich-Carolath was not so bright, although there are a few privately produced postcards to be found of a uniformed Kaiser, complete with decorations, arm-in-arm with his new bride.

For the ex-Kaiser, it seemed, life was still sweet, but for the majority of his countrymen 1922 was a financial nightmare. The mark dropped in exchange value in the Weimar Republic to 1,810 to the British pound; Rathenau, a distinguished man who had been appointed Minister of Reconstruction, had planned to free Germany of her wartime debts by inflating the currency, but his scheme to keep the mark at 300 to the pound was thwarted with his assassination in June 1922. Tight control had gone, and the ordinary German people were ruined. There are many cards depicting the misfortunes of Germany at that time: some are satirical cartoons; others are photographic arrangements showing bundles of worthless banknotes.

In 1922 archaeologist Howard Carter and Lord Carnarvon discovered the tomb of King Tutankhamun in the Valley of the Kings at Luxor. A story was passed round that anyone who touched the tomb would swiftly die – a superstition which was lent some substance by Lord Carnarvon's death the following year. But Press pictures and postcards showing Howard Carter packing the priceless hoard ready for exhibition around the world plainly dismissed the tale as credulous nonsense. Extensive sets of picture postcards illustrating the discovery of Tutankhamun's treasure could be purchased at the exhibitions.

In March that year Londoners went to the pictures to see D. W. Griffith's silent movie *Orphans in the Storm*, starring Dorothy and Lilian Gish. This film took eight months to make at a Long Island studio, and two-and-a-half tear-jerking hours to watch. The general verdict was that it was 'ever so sad – but worth seeing', and there were 'ever so sad' postcards taken from the stills of the film on sale in the foyer of the picture-houses where it was shown.

On top of Marconi House in the Strand the London 2LO station commenced broadcasting to the people in November 1922, and the BBC was born. A new category for present-day postcard collectors was born too, namely 'Wireless Postcards'. Since each 'wireless' set contained an unbelievable amount of wire, there were endless opportunities for newspaper and postcard cartoonists to make merry with the new invention. Broadcasting also brought a galaxy of fresh faces to the postcard gallery of portraits of theatrical entertainers.

It was also in 1922 that some disturbing photographic cards began to drift around the world from Italy, pictures of Benito Mussolini marching his Fascists through Rome – a strange change of face for a working-class lad who was noted for his vigorous Socialist thinking during the war.

1923

This was the year when the face of ex-Corporal Hitler was first glimpsed on postcards. For several years since the end of the First World War Adolf Hitler had been making a political nuisance of himself, declaiming his views against the German government, capitalists and the Jews in the beer gardens of Germany. On forming the National Socialist party he persuaded General Ludendorff to be his patron. His hero was Benito Mussolini, and he once observed that 'If Germany could be given a Mussolini, the people would kneel down and worship him.' Like Mussolini, he was partial to marches, but his plan to march from Munich to Berlin was thwarted by the Bavarian police. Hitler was charged with high treason and sent to jail in 1923, and there is at least one postcard example to show the Hitler arrogance before his trial.

In Britain there was a Royal wedding when the parents of Queen Elizabeth II, the Duke of York and Lady Elizabeth Bowes-Lyon, were married at Westminster Abbey – and another large selection of Royal wedding postcards found their way into postcard albums.

The year 1923 was also a fine one for British football. Two hundred thousand people crammed into the new Wembley Stadium for the first Wembley Cup Final match between West Ham United and Bolton Wanderers. With mobs climbing fences, barriers virtually useless, and the pitch invaded, there were plenty of lively scenes which found their way onto the fronts of picture postcards. The game did eventually take place, and Bolton Wanderers won by two goals to one.

It was a year of disaster in Japan, when several of her large cities were destroyed by an earthquake in which nearly a million people died. Pictures of this catastrophe were distributed by the news agencies, some of which were transferred to postcards.

On a happier note, there are the photographic cards of C. B. Cochran handing over a gold cup to Georges Carpentier after he had knocked out England's Joe Beckett at Olympia on 1 October. And radio dealers from London's East End came up with an enterprising advertising gimmick in the form of a three-wheeler car which they had fitted with radio. This little car, with its two loud-speakers, overhead aerial and the advertisements for 'Stratford Wireless' blazoned on its doors, toured the streets blaring out concerts to the passers-by, some of whom rushed home to fetch their cameras to photograph this forerunner of car radio. A number of these photographs were good enough for local printers to reproduce on postcards.

1924

At the end of 1923 Stanley Baldwin (the first politician to make pipe-smoking a symbol of prime ministerial respectability) was in trouble with his policy of Protection and Imperial preference.

His government fell, and he was defeated at the ensuing General Election. The consequent appearance of the first Labour government, headed by Mr Ramsay MacDonald, was an opportunity for another 'first' to be seen on social-history postcards. Out went the staid portrayals of sober-faced politicians, and in came an abundant supply of cards showing political informality, with the newly appointed ministers actually being caught with smiles on their faces.

In that same month of January 1924, while Ramsay MacDonald was enjoying his new role as Britain's first Socialist Prime Minister, the founder of Russian Socialism died. The body of Lenin, embalmed beneath glass, became a Soviet shrine, and there are many postcards to be found of the 'Red Saint' lying calm and serene in his death chamber.

Later that year a third attempt was made to conquer Mount Everest, and postcards were despatched by postal runners to India. All these cards showed a vignette of Mount Everest from the base camp in Rongbuk Valley, Tibet, and all were signed: 'Best Wishes – J. B. L. Noel, Captain, Mt Everest Expedition', beneath which was given the advance news that 'The Film of this great Exploit will be shown throughout the country, commencing at the Scala Theatre, London, November, 1924'.

But by far the most dominant event of 1924 was the official opening of the British Empire Exhibition at Wembley on St George's Day by King George V. There had been many previous exhibitions, but none could boast the splendour of the British Empire show. For one shilling and sixpence visitors could look forward to a fifteen-mile tramp of sightseeing through the great Palaces of Art and Industry and Engineering, on through the displays staged by eighteen Dominions and Colonies, and stop awhile to listen to one of the six daily concerts or admire the magnificent show of flowers. There were replicas of Tutankhamun's Tomb, of the Taj Mahal, and even of the mud huts of a West African village to see – as well as a two-and-a-half ton silver nugget and a million pounds worth of jewellery. And for children of all ages the forty acres of Amusement Park was a paradise of fun. There were special issues of British Empire Exhibition stamps designed by Harold Nelson to stick on the millions of postcards which could be purchased and posted on site, each card dated and franked with the Exhibition postmark. Most of the postcards were published by Fleetway Press Ltd, of Holborn, who described themselves as being the sole Concessionaires, but there were many other Exhibition cards by other publishers to buy from the stands and special kiosks, including some fine sets by Raphael Tuck and Sons Ltd.

1925

This was a centenary year for the railways, and particularly for the inhabitants of Teesside. George Stephenson's engine, which opened the world's first passenger railway – between Stockton and Darlington – in 1825, made the fourteen-mile journey again in July 1925 to celebrate its centenary. Filled with passengers

Figure 10. 100 years of railway achievement

wearing top-hats, it led a procession of engines and rolling stock of the 1920s to mark one hundred years of railway achievement. Two of the postcards which were issued for this occasion are shown in plates 43 and 44. (See also Figure 10.)

Cricket, too, had a good year in 1925, when Jack Hobbs delighted a crowd of ten thousand spectators on 17 August at Taunton, first by equalling W. G. Grace's record of one hundred and twenty six centuries, and the next day by making another century to beat the record. From then on Jack Hobbs was the subject of many gruelling photographic sessions for newspaper and postcard publishers.

The death of Queen Alexandra in November 1925 made the falling leaves of autumn more of a melancholy sight than usual. She was a most gracious and gentle lady who had been loved and respected by every class of the British people, and with her passing came ten thousand upon ten thousand of purple- and black-edged 'In Memoriam' postcards, and a regular output of cards to benefit the cause of hospitals continued to appear on every 'Alexandra's Rose Day', 26 June.

1926

This was one of the most exciting and active years for postcard publishers bent upon recording the events of the times.

Women's fashion was a controversial subject that year. To match the new short bobbed hair styles, skirts had also been creeping higher and higher, until by 1926 they had reached the immodest level of the knee, and dressmakers complained that they were on the brink of ruin now that dresses required a mere three yards of material instead of the customary seven! But women had no intention of giving up their breezy new freedoms, and the novel exposure of so many shapely legs provided a welcome bonus for postcard photographers.

Controversy had long raged over the propriety of jazz, but it did nothing to stop the Albert Hall being packed to capacity when Paul Whiteman and his jazz orchestra came to play, and the razzmatazz surrounding his welcome visit was not lost to postcards. From the exciting rhythms of jazz it was a short side-kick away to the shin-barking Charleston and the waggle of the Black-Bottom. These 'dances' were the scourge of 1926 ballrooms and were banned from many, but despite the bans and the tut-tutting from prim tight-lipped matrons the teenagers of the 1920s Charlestoned and waggled their nights away until the less energetic movements of the tango glided on to the dance floors. With the arrival of these new exercises, postcard publishers saw the potential of introducing features of the dance on cards, and some splendid ones, including artist-drawn sets, were issued throughout the remainder of the twenties and into the thirties.

July 24 1926 was the date when the first public greyhound race was run at the Manchester Belle Vue track, providing postcard publishers with yet another theme to keep the cash registers ringing.

At Wimbledon that year Betty Nuthall, a sixteen-year-old English girl, beat Mrs Mallory, eight times woman champion of the United States. But the defeat of Mrs Mallory at tennis was avenged by another American girl who became the first woman to swim the English Channel. Gertrude Ederle took fourteen hours and thirty-one minutes to swim from Cape Grisnez to Deal, and she beat the world record by one hour and fifty-nine minutes. So for that year sport on postcards was dominated by young Anglo-American female victories.

This was the year when Princess Elizabeth was born, and the heart-throb of the cinema, Rudolph Valentino, died. The traffic scene around London had a new attraction when the covered-top 'Generals' arrived to compete with the older type of omnibuses, the 'Spartans'. Hindenburg became President of Germany, and Anita Loos arrived from America to promote her book *Gentlemen Prefer Blondes*. And all of these events were reflected on postcards.

But not everyone shared the interest in the 'outrageous' fashions of women, or listened to jazz and learned to do the Charleston, for 1926 was also General Strike year in Britain. The whole of the work force ground to a halt at midnight on 3 May; the strike had begun, and it was total. Troops were brought in to transport and organize food supplies, vital services were kept going by thousands of volunteers, and the government published an official newspaper called the *British Gazette*. The General Strike was called by the Trade Union leaders in support of the miner's dispute over pay and conditions, and it lasted until 12 May. Although it did not achieve any joy for the miners, it emphasized the importance of the Trade Unions. Most postcards to be found featuring the activities during the General Strike were printed by small printers.

1927

Speed stole the headlines in 1927, when Major H. O. D. Segrave, in his car 'Golden Arrow', reached an average speed of 203.9 mph over Daytona Beach, Florida, and broke Malcolm Campbell's previous record of 174.22 mph. Plates 31 and 32, published by Selfridge & Co., are two of the postcards which registered this event.

On 20 May the American flyer Charles Lindbergh flew off into the night in an attempt to win the £5,000 prize offered for the first New York to Paris flight. His friends were decidedly pessimistic, declaring he would never make it. But on the following

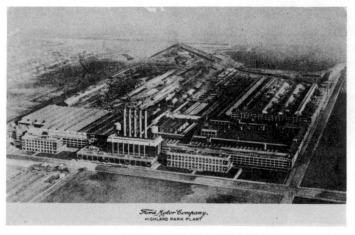

Figure 11. Ford's Highland Park Plant

47

day the message 'Captain Lindbergh arrived at Le Bourget Airdrome at 10.15 pm' was tapped out on the tape-machines, and Charles Lindbergh became yet another aviator to become immortal on postcards. A few days later he flew to Croydon where he was greeted by a hundred thousand cheering people, but the noisiest and craziest reception was in New York, where two million people lined the streets to have a look at 'Lindy', the flying marvel!

Henry Ford had a successful year. (See Figure 11.) His 'Tin Lizzie' model passed the fifteen million mark that year, and to celebrate the achievement there were some splendid publicity cards showing a close-up of the car with 'The Fifteen Millionth Ford' stretched across its doors. It was also the year when the new two-seater from Ford's was introduced at a cost of £145!

It was the year when Trotsky was banished from the Soviet Union by Joseph Stalin and exiled to Turkistan, and the year when the ex-Kaiser's sister married a twenty-seven year old Russian refugee. Today postcards of Soviet notabilities and their activities are highly collectable.

And in Britain this was the year when the first Greyhound Derby was run at the White City – which just went to prove how much 'going to the dogs' had caught on. In Britain coinage was given a new look by George Kruger Gray, and once again the Rose, the Thistle and the Shamrock were incorporated in the design. The British Post Office introduced the first automatic telephones, and Oxford Bags were considered to be the last word in sartorial elegance – possibly because of the postcards depicting the Prince of Wales wearing them!

1928

This was a year both of attainment and sad farewell. A year when the Equal Franchise Bill was passed which gave the 'Flapper's vote' to one-and-a-half million women aged between twenty-one and twenty-five in Britain. A year when the American Miss Amelia Earhart became the first woman to step into an aeroplane and risk the ordeal of flying the Atlantic. Four years later she undertook the first solo Transatlantic flight by a woman, from

Newfoundland to a field in Londonderry. The brave American lady well deserved all the tributes paid to her by the postcard publishers.

And this was a year when the world said farewell to so many famous people. In January 1928 Lord Haig died at the age of sixty-six. His funeral procession to Westminster Abbey stretched more than a mile long. Thomas Hardy also died in that January, and his ashes were buried in Poets' Corner at the Abbey. Henry Relph, who was so much better known by his stage name of Little Tich, died in February. At the height of his career this lovable little comedian had earned £450 a week, and yet he died without a penny to his name. He once observed: 'If ever you become top of the bill in the variety profession, you will be amazed at the number of poor relations you will have to help!' In June Emily Pankhurst, the founder of the Women's Suffrage movement, died at the age of sixty-eight, and during the following month Ellen Terry died, to make up a quintet who had stretched their gifts to the utmost and had known the love and respect of millions in return.

When *The Jazz Singer* was shown as the first feature-length talking picture, the English critics dismissed it as a freak. Al Jolson singing half-a-dozen songs and speaking a few lines did not constitute a talking film, they said, and to them the silent movie would always represent the true cinema. A year later they were forced to eat their words.

1929

The word-eating ceremony came after Al Jolson's next film was shown in 1929. *The Singing Fool* was an immediate success as a fully fledged 'talkie', and its hit song 'Sonny Boy' was whistled, hummed and sung by everybody. It also quickened the interest in the production of postcards depicting the new film-stars, and in this enterprise the regular postcard publishers were joined by the film-making companies and the specialist film magazines.

Since the end of the war London's theatreland had concentrated more on presenting bright, slick plays and musicals – possibly as an antidote to the heavy doses of wartime sentiment. But by 1929

Noël Coward believed that the time was ripe for something more romantic, and he set to work on a new musical play which incorporated the nostalgia of glamorous dress uniforms, beautiful dresses, glittering chandeliers and a romantic music score. Manchester was the first to see *Bitter Sweet* and hear 'I'll See You Again' (which became another perennial hit song); then London, and finally New York. Noël Coward's play and his leading lady Evelyn Laye broke all the records, and two more notabilities of the theatre were added to a long line of postcard 'greats' for the albums.

On Tuesday 29 October 1929 panic swept down Wall Street and through the stock markets of America. Millions of shares were put on the market, millions of dollars of paper profits were wiped out, and hundreds of suicides were reported. The American slump was the shattering result of over-production, the artificial fixing of commodity prices and too much credit. The gaiety of the 1920s had gone, and the American Depression had arrived.

1930

By the beginning of 1930 the cold winds of Depression were blowing over Britain, leading to the formation of a National Government in 1931. Even so, 1930 itself was crammed with events to attract postcard photographers, and some of them were none too pleasant. Adolf Hitler, for instance, won six million votes in the German elections of 1930 for his National Socialist party. This prompted the first Nazi postcards to be produced, and, with Dr Goebbels at Hitler's side, these were soon turned into colourful pieces of propaganda for the party.

Airships were in the news again. There were picture postcards of the Graf Zeppelin flying over the Wembley Stadium during the 1930 Cup Final, and others of the British airships R100 and R101 at their mooring masts. The R101 later exploded over Beauvais, France, with fifty-four passengers and crew abroad.

This was a year of triumph for woman aviator Amy Johnson, who flew alone from England to Port Darwin, Australia, and for the young Australian cricketer Don Bradman, who broke seven records during that year's Test series when Australia regained the

Ashes. It was a year of joy for the Duke and Duchess of York, when their second daughter, Princess Margaret Rose, was born.

Rich eccentrics were to the fore in 1930 – especially a financier who worked his way up from tea-boy to being controller of companies worth several million pounds. Martin Coles Harman bought the tiny island of Lundy in the Bristol Channel in 1925, and declared it to be an independent 'kingdom' with himself proclaimed as 'king'. The fifty or so Lundy inhabitants were not required to pay rates or taxes, and to add to the fun in 1927 the official versions of coins and stamps were replaced by special Lundy issues. The door was opened to this strange state of affairs when the official Post Office put up its shutters in 1927 after forty years of managing the postal business of the island. An arrangement was made whereby Martin Coles Harman undertook to carry the mail to the mainland, but it was not part of the arrangement for him to issue his own stamps and coins. The coins were known as puffins and half-puffins, one side bearing the head of a puffin, the other an engraving of the head of Martin Coles Harman surrounded by the inscription of his name, and the stamps were similar in design. But in 1930 the 'King' of Lundy Island was charged under the Coinage Act for issuing illegal coins. He was fined five pounds and fifteen guineas costs – and lost his appeal. Postcards and envelopes bearing the Lundy Puffin stamps are now valuable collectors' items.

*   *   *   *   *

The events covered in this chapter are a minute fraction of life as it was in the 1920s. There are many thousands of postcards to be found which illustrate local customs, pageants, activities, curiosities, industries and occupations, accidents and disasters and, like many of the more widely known affairs described here, the most interesting postcards of social history give no information about the photographers and printers who produced them. But of one thing collectors can be certain; the original supply of these 'anonymous' cards was very limited compared with those which were published by well-known manufacturers and, when they are found, they usually carry the price-tag of rarity!

3 *Some Postcard Best-Sellers of the Twenties*

During the inventive twenties the accent was on freedom and fun and changes for the better. Women who had swapped their skirts for trousers to do the jobs of men during the war were not to be persuaded to return to wearing long frocks over several petticoats when it was over, and the fashion for knee-length hem-lines was born. The heart-and-soul-searching melodies of wartime were drowned forever by the insistent beat of jazz; the exuberance of the Charleston upset the decorum of the dance floors, and nothing smelled so sweet as the heady scent of commercial and professional success.

Postcards immortalized every fashion, every fleeting fancy, every linchpin of mercantile triumph throughout the twenties and beyond and, far from dying away, filling postcard albums was a pastime pursued as ardently as ever. The fact that the cards of the 1920s were not as exquisitely printed as the pre-war variety bothered the postcard-buying public of those days not in the slightest. What mattered most was choice, and there was plenty of that – enough to fill several books, let alone this one short chapter, which must be confined to mentioning just a few of the best-selling postcard delights of the twenties.

A dog called Bonzo

In 1914 George Studdy drew a sketch of a dog with a sharp nose, a narrow jaw, and a spot on its rear hind quarters. He captioned this drawing 'The Late Tenant', and in time it appeared on his regular page in *The Sketch*. This unnamed dog continued to creep into Studdy's sketches in its lean and hungry fashion, and was featured in the 1920 Christmas number of *The Sketch* under the title 'Nipped in the Bud'. This version of the Bonzo yet to come showed the dog perched on a bucket of frozen water, his nose dripping from having just cracked the ice. Much later a postcard appeared of the same drawing, with the caption 'I've broken the ice!', which is just what George Studdy did when he fattened out his creation, crinkled its face, gave it a golf-ball nose and big feet, and called it Bonzo!

The publishers of *The Sketch* must have had a hunch that the new account of the Studdy dog would be a winner, but they could not have known that the drawings they commissioned for their portfolios would turn Bonzo into a cult. This funny little fable of George Studdy's imagination turned into a world-wide pheno-menon, and a talisman of commerce.

Cuddly Bonzos, clockwork Bonzos, celluloid Bonzos, pull-along Bonzos, Bonzos that rattled and Bonzos that squeaked kept the cash registers at the toy shops ringing for a decade and more. Bonzo ash-trays and pin-trays and trinket boxes and tea-sets vanished like snow in the sun from the china shops. Sweet and chocolate manufacturers turned their lollipops, jelly-babies, sugary fondants and chocolate bars into Bonzo shapes. Bookshops and stationers and art shops packed their shelves and adorned their walls with books and prints and calendars and a profusion of postcards. Even motor cars were considered to be improperly dressed without an impudent Bonzo mascot perched on their bonnets.

In an advertisement published by A. V. N. Jones and Co., 64 Fore Street, London, it was announced that thirty-one of the best Bonzo drawings had been made into jig-saw puzzles in satin wal-nut at a price of three shillings and sixpence each – a mere 17½p in today's currency. The same firm produced a number of pottery and porcelain items which carried the special registered trade mark 'Bonzo China Series', with a sketch of Bonzo sitting on a plate between the last two words. Nowadays all these Bonzo pro-ducts are viewed as highly collectable objects, and any which are still to be found outside private collections can be relied upon to be costly to purchase.

As far as Bonzo postcards are concerned, however, there is still enough scope for collectors of more modest means. From the early 1920s right up to the 1950s Bonzo cards were published by a number of postcard manufacturers throughout the world. The first to appear were issued in the RPS series; others were published by the Inter-Art Co., Florence House, Barnes, London in their 'Comique' range; but the main flow came from Valentine and Sons Ltd, of Dundee. There were also many French, German, Dutch, American, and Japanese Bonzos as well. In fact the Japanese welcomed the invention of this canine marvel with the extravagant toast '*Banzai Bonzo*', which was understood to mean that they could put up with him for ten thousand years!

It is difficult to say exactly how many different Bonzo postcards were published, but there are several collectors who are attempting to compile check-lists of the Valentine Bonzo cards. The most expensive postcards of Bonzo are those where he is to be seen promoting named products. One of the most coveted examples is the advertisement for the Wolseley Ten motor car. Bonzo is perched at the wheel of this fabulous model, which boasts a Bonzo mascot on its bonnet and the word Bonzo for a number-plate. The actual advertising part is so discreet as to be almost non-existent, with the caption 'SATISFIED AT LAST – Bonzo buys a Wolseley' minutely written in the bottom left-hand corner. This same discretion applies to the advertisement for Pascall's sweets, with the name merely appearing on the sweet jar Bonzo is lifting from the shelf. One of these esoteric advertising cards can be seen in Plate 140. At first glance it looks as though Bonzo is on his way to a 'bring your own drink' party; a second look might suggest a promotion for soda-siphons and beers; a closer scrutiny – possibly with a magnifying glass – reveals the words 'Excelsior-Reifen' written on the tyre rims!

Mabel Lucie Attwell postcards

While Bonzo was spreading his canine brand of enchantment around the world, long hard looks were being focused on the work of another important artist. Mabel Lucie Attwell was already as well known for her drawings of children as George Studdy was for his animals. During the First World War Mabel Lucie drew hundreds of sketches of blue-eyed tots with rosebud mouths and petal-pink cheeks for the *Bystander*, and Valentine and Sons Ltd, of Dundee, produced a host of postcards depicting the endearing innocence of her creations. Many of these wartime cards found their way into the trenches, to be pinned up alongside the glamorous French enchantments.

After the war it was not long before someone recognized the potential of the Attwell children for becoming a 'hot commercial property', although there was not quite the build-up for them as there was for the Bonzo craze. Perhaps this was because they were essentially feminine, while Bonzo appealed to both sexes. But there was a huge market for 'Attwell' books and games, handkerchiefs and tea-towels, ornaments and nursery crockery, and the endless selection of postcards and decorated stationery on display in the shops.

Valentine continued to be Mabel Lucie Attwell's major publisher, and it is interesting to note how the reverse side of the Attwell postcards changed during the years of her immense popularity. In wartime, Attwell cards had simply stated 'Valentine Series', but in the 1920s this was altered to 'Valentine's ATTWELL series', followed either by the words 'Copyright picture' or 'Copyright. Valentine & Sons Ltd'. By the 1930s Valentine's took the unusual step of declaring 'ALL GENUINE ATTWELL POSTCARDS HAVE THE ARTIST'S SIGNATURE THUS:' followed by a facsimile of how Mabel Lucie Attwell signed her work. The reason for this could well have been the prolific crop of other postcards which were published during this period by artists whose work closely resembled the famous Attwell children.

Mabel Lucie Attwell was very much a woman of her time – and sometimes ahead of it. She anticipated the universal craze for Art Deco by a good few years, as can be seen in Plate 168. This is a card which was published by Valentine and postmarked 1919, and shows a more slender version of the Attwell child wearing high boots, a chequered Art Deco dress and a sun-ray striped hat. There are a number of Attwell postcards which have a distinct touch of the Art Deco about them – especially those published after 1925.

This thoroughly modern lady always kept her 'children' well informed and in the height of fashion, and almost always the captions and the pictures reflected the moods and social topics of the time.

Social history recorded on nursery postcards

Plates 130–35 demonstrate how the social topics of the twenties were incorporated into the sketches that featured children. A browse through the dealers' boxes marked 'Children' can still produce a fair crop of cards worth including among the more orthodox types of social history, to leaven a collection. (Figure 12 reflects the new interest in air travel, as drawn by Nora Annie Birch.)

A cat called Felix

The little black cat with a white face, who could never stop walking, was created by the Australian Pat Sullevan. Felix first started his perambulations in 1917, and later he captivated audiences when he starred in the short 'Felix the Cat' animated cartoons. Among the many postcards to feature Felix were those published by Woolstone Brothers of London, in their 'Milton' series, and reproductions from *Pathé's Eve*, *Everybody's* and the *Film Review* magazines were published by the Inter-Art Co. of Barnes, London.

A mouse called Mickey

Towards the end of the 1920s Felix the Film Cat was taunted by a mouse – for one of the most famous cartoon characters was to arrive upon the film scene at this time. In 1928 Walt Disney's creation 'Mickey Mouse' starred in the first cartoon 'talkies', *Steamboat Willie* and *Plane Crazy*, and again the imagination of postcard publishers was captured.

'Mickey Mouse' skipped and danced over the surface of a great

Figure 12. A nursery postcard

number of cards published in the United States, Germany, France and Britain – a German version can be seen in Plate 150. Inter-Art Co. produced many of the early British 'Mickey' cards, and Valentine and Sons Ltd reproduced a long and colourful series in the 1950s which included many of the other Disney characters as well.

And a monkey called Gran'pop

Valentine and Sons were also the publishers of the long 'Gran'pop' series. Gran'pop was a wise old monkey created by Lawson Wood, who drew his cartoons from life rather than from his imagination.

The ideas for Gran'pop continued to entertain both buyers of postcards and audiences of animated cartoon films right up until the 1950s.

The crossword puzzle craze

Although the *first* crossword puzzle, compiled by Arthur Wynne of Liverpool, was published in the *New York World* in December 1913, it was eleven years before the British were introduced to the joys of solving newspaper crosswords. The first to appear was published in the *Sunday Express*, on 2 November 1924, and it was not until 1 February 1930 that solving the puzzle in *The Times* became a status symbol of national one-upmanship! But in the 1920s the world became crossword crazy and established an institution as firm as the Rock of Gibraltar – and a new theme for postcards. Raphael Tuck and Sons Ltd produced two coveted sets called 'The Crossword Craze', and Plate 148 shows one of the 'Cross Word Puzzle' cards produced by Millar & Lang.

Glossy greetings postcards

While most of the more seasoned postcard collectors acknowledge the existence of glossy greetings cards with a superior sniff, the less 'well informed' are filled with rapturous delight at the sight of the deckle-edged bowers of flowers designed to commemorate important occasions for every known relative and friend. The less well informed laymen could be proved to be rather more astute in their judgement than their better informed fellows – after all, the popularity of merchandise in any field depends upon the verdict of the public. Even before the 1920s the glossy greetings card had become an integral part of the world's anniversary celebrations, and postcard publishers had found a rich store of jam to go with the bread and butter provided by their productions of view cards. Glossy greetings were published in their trillions – and became too common to be worth a second's consideration by serious postcard collectors, a fate which would have been shared by cards signed by Mucha or Kirchner as well, had they too been produced on such a scale! It could well be that in the years to come these mainstays of the greetings card departments of Woolworths and other big stores will yet be called into the collecting fold, but until that day arrives they can still be purchased for a minimum of pence.

Apart from the countless photographs in glossy sepia which were produced by Hollywood's film companies of the bright young stars of the cinema scene (see Figure 13), there were many others

GRETA GARBO   METRO-GOLDWYN-MAYER PICTURES

Figure 13. Greta Garbo in *Anna Christie*

to be seen which followed the well-tried formula of the glossy greetings. J. Beagles produced a long and successful run of such cards in their 'Famous Cinema Stars' series, and De Reszke, the cigarette people, issued a long series of coloured photographs of film stars in the larger packages of their cigarettes – examples from these series can be seen in plates 154 and 155. There was no doubt that the craze for collecting cards of every known face to flit across the screens of the cinema in the 1920s was every bit as fervent as the fad for collecting the photographs of Edwardian actors and actresses in pre-war days, and of course some of the younger stars of the Edwardian theatre went on to join the galaxy of the cinema firmament. One such young star was Gladys Cooper, who was not only the photographer's idea of the perfect model and a very fine actress, but an avid collector of postcards as well!

Novelty postcards of the 1920s

As well as the well-tried views and glossy greetings, publishers continued to produce an enormous choice of concertina novelty cards. These are the cards with the tantalizing pictures which promise all sorts of strange delights hidden under the flap of concertina pull-out strips. But the invitations to discover 'What I found under my bed at Blackpool', or wherever, usually end up with the sight of a dozen sepia views in miniature of the Town Hall, the Gas Works and other places of municipal pride.

Valentine & Sons reintroduced the American idea of 'Klever Kards' when they published their 'Cut-Out Motto Cards' series. A Mabel Lucie Attwell example is shown in Figure 14 and on the reverse of this card are the instructions to 'cut through the connecting bridges of the design, fold back at the dotted line, so as to enable the card to stand up'. 'Alpha' started a craze for glass-eyed cards, which mostly featured cats and parrots, but there were also a number of glass-eyed children, and sophisticated versions of flirtatious gentlemen with moving eyes. E. T. W. Dennis produced many of the popular lever-change cards with tabs to pull to change the action of the picture. W. H. Smith and Son created the 'X-Ray Illusion Postcard' which showed a skeleton hand with a hole in the middle; viewers were invited to place the hole to the eye with one hand and place the other twelve inches in front when the bones of that hand would be seen. An incredible illusion resulted, guaranteed to bring gasps of horror from every viewer who saw the gelatinous appearance of what looked like his very own bones. Then there were the 1920s versions of cards sprinkled with glitter, appliquéd with velvets and ginghams, tinted photographs of ladies in cloche hats decorated with real feathers, and donkey barometers with woolly tails. And at the seaside holiday resorts there were kiosks where holidaymakers

KEEP ME AS A MASCOT PROPER
AN' YOU'LL NEVER LACK A COPPER!

Figure 14. A 'Cut-Out Motto Card'

could make novelties of themselves by poking their heads through a hole in a board to complete an array of headless forms which ranged from scantily clad fat ladies to soberly dressed clergymen. These hilarious sights were then photographed, and converted into cards to send to the folks back home. (See Figure 15.)

Raphael Tuck and Sons came up with many splendid ideas for novelty postcards during the twenties, including a number of fascinating cards for children in their 'Pastime' series. There were dolls and furniture and model railway engines and flowers to cut out and assemble into stand-up models, and there were sets of birds and butterflies with perforated wings to press into flying positions, and another range of jig-saw puzzle postcards to amuse on rainy days. Obviously these cards for the children are rare finds in pristine condition today: they were, after all, meant to be

Figure 15. A novelty postcard

played with, and the children of the 1920s took the fullest advantage of them.

Enchanting 'children' cards of the 1920s

From very early in postcard history there had been a constant flow of artistic renderings of the world of the child, and there was no slackening of interest or pace in the twenties. Among the most delightful of these cards were those drawn by artists like Susan Pearse, Millicent Sowerby, Lilian Govey, Hester Margetson, Chloe Preston and Dorothy Wheeler, and published by Humphrey Milford of London. The tradition of Milford excellence was continued by Henry Frowde & Hodder and Stoughton when Humphrey Milford went to the Oxford University Press in the mid-1920s. (See Figure 16, artist Susan Pearse.)

HOME·FROM·THE·PARTY
WE HAD A SIMPLY SPLENDID TEA,
OUR SUPPER, TOO, WAS HEARTY,
BUT HOME WE WALK QUITE FAST, YOU SEE,
AFTER OUR CHRISTMAS PARTY!

Figure 16. 'Christmas Time'

C. W. Faulkner & Co. Ltd published many sets of appealing children which included work by Helen Jacobs, Hilda Miller and Joyce Mercer, whose postcards are now just as coveted by collectors of Art Deco. Then there are the sets of cards drawn by Agnes Richardson and produced by Raphael Tuck and Sons Ltd, who also published the vividly coloured sketches on a black background by Phyllis Cooper. And from another famous postcard publisher, A. & C. Black Ltd, came the enchanting sets of 'Elves and Fairies' by Ida Rentoul Outhwaite, 'English Nursery Rhymes' by Dorothy Wheeler, and more nursery rhymes by Charles Folkard, the creator of the Teddy Tail cartoons which were published in the *Daily Mail*.

Dolls' Houses and Palaces fit for a Queen

The idea for building and furnishing the Queen's Dolls' House to present to Queen Mary was first conceived in 1920. Presided over by architect Sir Edwin Lutyens, the project emerged as a jewel of combined craftsmanship in time for showing at the British Empire Exhibition, where it became one of the major attractions. A complete inventory of the contents of this fabulous house was published in Volume One of *The Book of the Queen's*

Dolls' House by the *Daily Telegraph*, with a full list of Donors, Artists, Makers and Craftsmen.

The House itself – which is now one of the tourist attractions inside Windsor Castle – stands thirty-nine inches high on a base measuring one hundred and sixteen inches by seventy-two inches, and inside every beautifully decorated room is a wealth of miniature beauty and invention. Of special interest to postcard collectors are the prints to be seen in the Library of George Studdy's 'Bonzo', Will Owen's 'Somebody's Darling', F. G. Lewin's 'Blackberry Jam Piccaninny', Frank Reynolds' 'Mr Punch and Toby' and 'Listening-In' by Percy Fearson (Poy).

To commemorate the gift to Queen Mary of the Queen's Dolls' House, Raphael Tuck produced forty-nine postcards in six sets. These cards were on sale at the British Empire Exhibition and sold either in single sets or in special albums or boxes. Profits from the sale of the cards went to the QDH Charitable Fund, which was administered by Queen Mary and shared among the many worthy causes which were dear to her heart. Plate 190 illustrates 'The King's Bedroom' from Series Three of the Tuck QDH cards, and the full check-list of this very important series of postcards is listed as follows:

Oilette No. 4500 – Series One
1. Dining Room Sideboard
2. Hall Table and Chairs
3. China Coffee Service
4. Dining Room
5. Entrance Hall
6. Garden Entrance
7. Dining Room Fireplace
8. Wine Cellar

Oilette No. 4501 – Series Two
1. Drawing Room Cabinet
2. The Library
3. Regalia in Strong Room
4. Corner of the Library

5. The King's Library Table
6. Grand Piano in Drawing Room
7. Some of the Drawing Room furniture
8. Some of the Library furniture

Oilette No. 4502 – Series Three

1. Wardrobe and Chest of Drawers in the Queen's Apartment
2. The King's Bedroom (illustrated)
3. The Queen's Bed
4. Princess Royal's Bedroom
5. The King's Bathroom
6. The Queen's Bathroom
7. Some of the Furniture in the Queen's Bedroom
8. The Queen's Bedroom
9. The Drawing Room of the Queen's Dolls' House

Oilette No. 4503 – Series Four

1. In the Linen Room
2. Carpet in the Queen's Bedroom
3. Chinese Cabinet in the Queen's Bedroom
4. Her Majesty's Dressing Table
5. Gold Chest with Gold Tea and Coffee Service
6. Writing Desk and Chair in the Queen's Bedroom
7. Her Majesty's Boudoir
8. Fireplace and Overmantel in the Queen's Bedroom

Oilette No. 4504 – Series Five

1. China Tea Service and Toilet Set
2. The Royal Nursery – Cradle, Baby Chair and Weighing Machine
3. The Royal Kitchen
4. The Royal Nursery
5. The Kitchen Table
6. Nursery Toys
7. Nursemaid's Closet
8. Nursery Piano and Gramophone

Oilette No. 4505 – Series Six

1. Safety First, The Fire Escape
2. Garage showing the Interior of Rooms above
3. Guns, Punch Bowl, Screen and Stick Stand
4. Games, Croquet, Cricket, Golf and Tennis
5. Perambulator and Motorcycle
6. Stores and Provisions in the Cellar
7. The Electric Light and Water Systems
8. Complete Model of the House and Garden.

This check-list gives only the bare essentials for identifying each card; the cards themselves have to be seen to enjoy the exquisite detail of many of the items which are shown, all of them made with care and love by the craftsmen and artists to whom J. C. Squire paid tribute in his 'Acrostic Sonnet on the Queen's Dolls' House':

This is the house a thousand artists made,
Honouring a lady with the things they wrought.
Each of his love and cunning craft brought
Queen Mary tribute, in this house displayed.
Upon this house a thousand fancies strayed,
Ephemeral fancies, painting on a page
Eternal symbols of one dreaming age,
Numbering all the toys with which we played.
Suns rise and set, the flowers fade and we
Here will men find, when still are all the hands
Once busy in these rooms, in stranger days,
Us, and the common habit of our ways,
Safer than Pharaohs buried in their sands,
Enshrined in open day, to all posterity.

(Reproduced from *The Queen's Dolls' House* book, published by the *Daily Telegraph*.)

From the perfection of the Queen's Dolls' House we move on to the excellence of 'Titania's Palace', created by the hands of one man, Major Sir Neville Wilkinson, who spent some twenty years building the Palace, and thirty years to fill its sixteen rooms with ten thousand miniatures of ancient and modern art. In 1922 Titania's Palace was opened to the public by Queen Mary, and after a while it was taken on tour around the world to enchant countless children. Raphael Tuck published two sets of eight cards each to illustrate the exterior and interior of Titania's Palace, and again all the profits went to help charitable causes.

To complete the trilogy of miniature palaces and houses, Tuck also published two sets, one in sepia and one in colour, to illustrate 'Mirror Grange', the house built by the *Daily Mirror* for their loveable trio of characters 'Pip, Squeak and Wilfred'.

St Valentine's Day postcards

In the nineteenth century February 14th was a day of great excitement for young Victorian ladies, when they received their share of St Valentine tokens. These could be in the form of cheques and drafts made out to Hymen's Temple, the Bank of Love etc., or they could be in the form of the delicate, lacy creations which are illustrated in Frank Staff's excellent book *The Valentine and Its Origins*. But the young ladies of the 1920s were denied such pleasures until Lady Adolph Tuck persuaded her husband to reintroduce them. To authenticate this charming story an extract from the booklet *The Romance of the House of Raphael Tuck and Sons Ltd*, which was published jointly by Tuck and Fine Arts Development Ltd, on the occasion of the Company's centenary in October 1966, is quoted here:

In 1925 Lady Tuck was discussing with her husband the firm's Diamond Jubilee, which would come the following year. She suggested that they should celebrate the occasion by reviving a charming custom that had fallen into disuse since the early part of the century – St Valentine cards.

For St Valentine's Day 1926 the House of Tuck revived the Valentine and scored an immediate success which has not only been maintained to this day but has greatly increased on both sides of the Atlantic.

This revival was the last of Sir Adolph's many pioneering

enterprises. He died in July of that year and was succeeded to the title by his eldest son Reginald.

From then on, all manner of Valentine cards from many different publishers appeared in the postcard racks in good time for posting on St Valentine's Eve.

And so to Art Deco on postcards

Art Deco design was originally unveiled in the studios of fashionable couturiers at the beginning of the twentieth century. The characteristic style in those days was a combination of the inspired use of Oriental Art with geometrical symmetry, and the startling use of brash, bright colours. Some of the great names to appear on postcards which displayed the early Art Deco influence were those of fashion artists such as Paul Iribe, Pierre Brissaud, Lucien Vogel, A. E. Marty, Thayart and Leon Bakst who also designed the costumes and decor for Diaghilev's 'Ballets Russes'. Throughout the days of the war and into the 1920s, the movement of Art Deco continued to increase in importance, until it exploded into a world-wide craze in the mid-twenties.

Suddenly the world took a giant leap into an age which was dominated by great splashes of brilliantly clashing colours which somehow never set the teeth on edge; designs which happily mixed polka dots with zig-zag stripes and checks with rising sun-rays; mad, mad furniture, chromium-plated lamps, square tea-pots, and crockery by Clarice Cliff and Susie Cooper. Women danced along in beaded dresses with zig-zagged hem-lines and little cloche hats which completely covered their newly shingled hair styles. Art Deco of the twenties had travelled a long way from the original concept of the first devotees. The serious successor to the gentle curves and swirls of Art Nouveau had been snatched by the people and turned into a symbol of revolt against the whale-boned convention of the Mrs Grundy's of pre-war times.

Postcard artists were quick to capture the rebellious spirit of the new age, and for several years the flamboyant bewitchment of Art Deco adorned the postcard racks in every part of the world. Plates 166–83 show a fair example of the different styles, from the cheerful arguments in colour by Chloe Preston and Freda Mabel Rose to the flair of pure Art Deco by artists such as Mela Koehler, Nashnyekov, Chiostri and Montedoro, and a study of the plate descriptions will disclose the pleasant fact that not all Art Deco cards are in the pocket-breaking class!

*   *   *   *   *

These outlines of some of the best-selling postcards of the 1920s are just a fragment of the enticing choice which was available to the public at that time. Postcard publishers were as busy as ever they were – and the album manufacturers were not exactly idle either. There had been a breathless moment or two after the war when interest in collecting picture postcards appeared to be fading, but old habits die hard and by the dawn of the twenties there was a renewed enthusiasm for collecting pasteboard reflections of the times, and for this present-day collectors must surely be grateful. The essence, after all, of a true postcard collection lies in its nostalgia value and in the continuity of recording past events and fashions. The evidence portrayed by the postcards of the 1920s describes most colourfully the way things were.

4 *Behind the Sketchbook and Easel*

Whether it be for profit or pleasure, the game of palette and brush, like any other pursuit, needs practice, and the artists of picture postcards were given liberal scope to practise their skills in design. Artist-signed cards have long been one of the favourite collecting themes, and a natural sequel to owning these paintings in miniature is a curiosity about the lives and backgrounds of the men and women who painted them.

To satisfy this interest a number of articles appear from time to time in the postcard periodicals about some of the better-known artists, and these encourage an interest in many of the other people whose signatures are to be found on postcards, which stimulates collectors to pursue their own researches. Such sallies into the research field need patience, determination, and plenty of time to haunt museums and libraries and other likely archives of art and design records, and it is amazing how often desirable information pops up to dazzle the eye and race the pulse! Achieving and collating such information brings an enormous sense of satisfaction, as one discovers yet another dimension to a hobby already bulging with interest and surprises.

In these days of nostalgia cults, postcard collectors and their collections have more than most to offer, and while photographic postcards of the doings of bygone days show the reality of a moment the artistic impressions of the times so often reveal more about attitudes and emotions that bubble behind the scenes, not least the postures and singularity of the artists themselves.

To be able to translate thoughts or reflect a mood on paper or canvas with the sweep of a brush and the caress of a pen is an enviable gift, a gift which is usually recognized by those to whom it is given as a passport into worlds which give truth to the most outrageous fantasy. The small child earnestly filling the pages of his sketchbook commits to paper the sights of his own imagination, completely oblivious of whatever may be going on around him. The result of his efforts may be a bit bizarre for adult taste, but the child has drawn truth as he sees it, and if he has even a remote talent, the truth of that too will soon begin to shine and demand encouragement.

Delving back into the childhood of many of the postcard artists reveals a yearning for careers in the art world from a very early age, and, as some of the following biographical outlines show, the early road to recognition was often barred by parental disapproval.

Georges Henri Hautot

In 1887, at Fermanville, Manche, Georges Hautot was born. His father was a sailor, and as a small boy young Georges would entertain his friends by drawing boats in the sands near his home. Later, at school, his passion for drawing and his obvious artistic talent did not go unnoticed by his art teachers, and throughout his schooldays he was never dislodged from first place in the subject. Quite clearly, Hautot had visions of a blissful life following his artistic inclinations, but, equally clearly, he had reckoned without the wrath of his father. After only two months of studying at the Julian Academy, Hautot senior returned from one of his sea trips and forced his son to leave his art training to do a 'proper job' with the much respected but unexciting Post Office Administration. Georges Hautot jogged through this humdrum existence until he was twenty-six. He was now old enough to slip the halter of parental discipline and devote himself entirely to the work he really loved, which predominantly included his ambition to become a magazine illustrator. By 1915 he was a regular contributor to journals such as *Le Matin*, *La Vie Parisienne*, *Le Rire* and *Fantasio*, as well as illustrating books and advertising posters, and many of these illustrations were reproduced on postcards. For relaxation he indulged his passion for the countryside by taking himself off with his easel and paint-box to camp in the fields and paint calm, gentle landscapes. But perhaps the most famous of Hautot's work to be seen on postcards are the First World War 'Army Cook' sketches depicting a French soldier character, which became as popular in France as Bruce Bairnsfather's creation of 'Old Bill' did in Britain.

Federico Ribas

Here was a man who was not to be thwarted – quietly acquiescent to his parents' wishes during the day, while teaching himself to paint and sculpt at night. When he was sent to Madrid to train for a respectable career it was not long before his artistic leanings took over and persuaded him to study drawing.

When Federico was seventeen years of age he left Madrid for Buenos Aires, where he scraped a living painting walls and doors, reserving all his spare time for the more aesthetic uses of paint and brush. It was not long before he was supplying illustrations to the magazine *Papel y Tinta*, rapidly earning for himself the reputation of being a first-class designer. This success was followed by commissions to work for other Argentine journals. During the First World War Ribas based himself in Paris and drew war sketches for his magazine contacts, some of which were reproduced on postcards. After the war his career took another turn. He entered a poster competition in Barcelona and landed the first prize, which led to his appointment as Art Director of La Perfumeria Gal in Madrid. Ribas had arrived! He devoted ten hours a day to the artistic and publicity management of his perfumery firm, including a daily stint of drawing a new creation to advertise its products on posters and postcards. His spare time was spent designing book covers and posters and postcards for outside concerns. The secret of his success was his insistence that his advertising work, as well as being essentially beautiful and strikingly colourful, should tell the public clearly and precisely what it was that was advertised. Postcards signed by this Spanish artist are more likely to be seen in European countries, where they are highly valued.

René Vincent

Another artist whose poster-type postcards are greatly prized is Bordeaux-born René Vincent. His father, Charles Vincent, was the French novelist who wrote under the *nom-de-plume* of Pierre Mael. With this background young René was fortunate, in that an early interest was taken in the talents he was showing in his drawing books, but fond parental imagination did not stretch further than the thought of their son becoming a brilliant draughtsman, perhaps even an architect. Hopeful of this eventual attainment, René Vincent was sent to work for M. André Destailleur in his architect's office. For eight years René spent his time copying endless plans and specifications, and whenever he had a spare minute he would use it to train himself to adapt his drawing ability to other techniques. His dream was to be a book illustrator, and when he felt that he was capable of producing presentable work he left the architect's employ to draw a series of sketches for 'Gyp's Novels', a series which was soon to receive enormous acclaim. From this triumph René Vincent progressed to be recognized as one of the foremost poster and publicity postcard artists in France.

Armand Massonet

Belgian artist Massonet was allowed to take his art seriously right from the moment of grasping his first pencil. His student days were varied and extensive: from the École Normale he graduated to the St Gilles Academy, from there to the Brussels Academy, and finally to the École Nationale des Beaux Arts in Paris; and wherever he went he was the one to pick up the most glittering prizes for his drawings.

His studies completed, and with so many honours tucked under his belt, he had every reason to look forward to the beginning of an immediately successful career, but the First World War interfered, and Massonet had to wait until it was over before taking the commercial art world by storm. During the war he served as a stretcher-bearer, and in his off-duty hours he assembled and published an art paper called *Le Claque à Ford*, despite being in the front line!

After the war he was installed as painter to the Art Section of the Army. The war had left its mark on Massonet, and many of his posters – which were later reproduced on postcards – depicted the plight of the wounded. His compassion was tremendous.

In the 1920s he became professor of drawing at three Brussels schools, wrote a book on sketching, contributed a variety of illustrations to a number of magazines and newspapers, and was commissioned by the Belgian Government to draw posters for such events as the Brussels Fair, Cardinal Mercier's fund and other charitable affairs. Much of this work was recorded on postcards.

Ludwig Kainer

Born in Munich in 1885, Ludwig Kainer's propensity for drawing became clear when he was only four years old, but it was not the parental intention that he should grow up to be an artist. After his formal education at grammar school he went to University to study medicine for a couple of years, and on to the Institut Pasteur in Paris, where he worked as a bacteriologist. But he still had the urge to paint and draw, and after a year or two he abandoned medicine for art.

His main interest was in the theatre, designing scenery and costumes for the ballet and the opera, and he published a number of albums of his designs. Needless to say Kainer's work, with its distinct art nouveau flair, found its way on to postcards. 'Le Ballet Russe', 'Dancers between New York and Bombay' and 'Nijinsky, the Dancer' are some of the titles to have been seen on cards. Most of his time was spent in Paris, but he had a particular love for New York, where he designed many settings for shows, including one for the Ziegfield Follies.

Maurice Millière

Millière was born at Le Havre in 1871, and while he was still a child it became obvious that the brush and palette were to be the tools of his trade. At the École des Beaux Arts he worked under

M. Bonnat, from whom he learned that perfection in the art of drawing is simplicity.

Later he became well known in the United States for his regular contributions to a number of New York, Philadelphia and Milwaukee journals. He was also one of the principal contributors to *Le Sourire* and *La Vie Parisienne*. During the First World War Millière drew a remarkable series of engravings of 'Life at the Indian Camp' (of Rouen) which were later exhibited at the Musée de L'Armée des Invalides. He was also the illustrator of many of the saucy glamour postcards which did so much to cheer up the troops during those war years.

Perhaps the most extensive series of postcards for which Maurice Millière was famous was his 'Petites Femmes de Paris'. Millière disliked trusting to memory, so all these sketches were drawn from living models, representing all levels of society, from the midinette to the languid society beauty.

Serge Goursat (S.E.M.)

For some reason best known to himself, this artist preferred the anonymity of the mysterious initials S.E.M. as a signature to his name of Serge Goursat. Born in Périgueux in the Dordogne in 1863, there is little to mention about his early years. After graduating as Bachelor of Science, he managed a shop in his home town for some fifteen years before moving to Bordeaux, then to Marseilles, and finally to Paris. Here he developed his flair for caricature, and specialized in sketching the rich and famous. Wherever his quarry went S.E.M. would follow; while they danced and dined and drank champagne in fashionable restaurants he would be sitting at a little table, sketching on bits of paper hidden beneath a table napkin. Another of his favourite haunts for catching society unawares was the race course, and he became a familiar figure to be seen at Newmarket races. Of his first visit there he tells an amusing story about himself. He was looking around for a 'subject' when he spotted Lord Lonsdale (although he was not then aware of who he was). Pencil and notebook in hand, he followed his illustrious quarry, concentrating only on his model. Lord Lonsdale was heading for the Royal Enclosure, and so was S.E.M., but not for long. Suddenly his collar was caught in a business-like grip, and he was propelled with great hustle to the Stewards' Office. There he stood, a little chap in a lounge suit and a bowler among all the toppers and morning coats, unable to speak one word of English. His movements were viewed with the utmost suspicion, and the dreaded word 'anarchist' was already going the rounds when Lord Howard de Walden came to his rescue and escorted him to the paddock. But this adventure was not so ill a wind, for Lord Lonsdale and the Aga Khan became the first of his willing subjects on that occasion, and later a number of the English racing cartoons were published on postcards.

He also exhibited a series of cut-out figures at the New Bond Street Fine Art Gallery, an exhibition which so delighted the British Royal Family that the whole collection was purchased and transferred to Sandringham.

After the war S.E.M. resumed publishing his portfolios of sketches and introduced a new series entitled 'Le Nouveau Monde'. Postcards signed by S.E.M. are at a premium, and he was one of the celebrated artists whose work was included in the desirable French series, 'Collection des Cent'.

Emil Orlik

This Prague-born artist drew a long series of sketch-portraits of famous composers: life studies of people such as Gustav Mahler, Anton Brüchner, Richard Strauss and Fritz Kreisler. These postcard illustrations came from Orlik's book entitled *95 Heads*, and at least fifty of them were reproduced for postcard purposes. There are also some Japanese cards to be found which were taken from his illustrated portfolio *Aus Japan*.

Harold Nelson

Collectors of advertising cards will immediately recognize this artist for his symbolic drawings for Dewar's whisky and Gordon Selfridge, and postal history devotees will know that it was Harold Nelson who designed the commemorative stamp for the 1924 British Empire Exhibition.

This modest man, born at Dorchester in 1871, worshipped all forms of nature, especially trees – which makes his choice of geometric symbolism in his art all the more surprising, until it is understood that he developed his liking for symbolic and decorative art by his study of the work of Albrecht Dürer. His art education began at the Lambeth School of Art and ended under Luke Taylor at the Central School for Arts and Crafts.

Many of his advertising drawings appeared on postcards, and a number of his book illustrations were similarly reproduced. There were delightful postcards from 'Undine' and 'Easter Joy', to 'The Talking Beasts', to mention a few.

Edward Hynes

Unlike most of the artists already mentioned, Edward Hynes did not discover his talent for caricature until he had served his time as a naval cadet, served as a navigation officer, and studied to become a doctor. All this activity took up many years of the life of this son of an Irish surgeon, before he ceased to dither between the call of medicine and the pull of the sea. The luck of the Irish, however, must have been his constant companion, for no sooner did he decide to convert his doodling style into professional cartoonism, than he was snapped up as a regular contributor to such newspapers as the *Daily Sketch*, the *Sunday Express* and the *Evening News*, and magazines like the *Bystander* and the *Sporting and Dramatic News*. The distinctive work of Hynes is none too easy to find on postcards, but in some rare collections the hallmark of the chap who could turn a question-mark into a masterpiece of cartoonery are to be seen. All the postcards are black and white line drawings, and include caricatures of people such as Sir William Orpen, George Grossmith and Sir John Lavery.

Kurt Heiligenstaedt

When he was only five years old this native of Rossleben began to sketch the picturesque corners of Thüringen. After leaving school he worked as an office clerk during the day, and used his evenings and weekends to perfect his ability for drawing. As soon as he came of age he left the office work behind him to go to the Berlin Academy for a course of formal art training. Progress there was too slow for his taste, however, so he discharged himself in favour of self-teaching. The war came to interrupt this enterprise, and it was not until after the war had ended that he first began to taste the sweet fruits of success. In addition to becoming one of the main contributors to the *Berliner Lustige Blätter*, he was also invited to work for *Jugend, Simplicissimus*, and other illustrated papers. Some of the contributions appeared on postcards, but ultimately Kurt Heiligenstaedt became far better known for his work in the advertising field.

Piet Van der Hem

A Dutch artist, born in Wirdum in Frise, Piet Van der Hem was another child who was to be allowed to follow his own artistic inclinations. He became a student at the Amsterdam School of Arts, and went on to Paris to perfect his ability and technique. His first job was his appointment as cartoonist for *De Groene Amsterdammer*, and later he was invited to supply a weekly front-page cartoon for *De Haagsche Post*. His specialist interest was drawing international political cartoons, and postcards are to be found of Van der Hem's renderings of the Kaiser in wartime, the Franco-Spanish situation in Morocco, Chinese problems, and the antics of British politicians. He was also commissioned to paint portraits of the Dutch Royal Family.

Ludwig Hohlwein

Hohlwein is another artist who began his career in an architect's office, where he stayed for three years. The Technical High School at Munich was his next port of call, and thanks to his professor, who introduced him to Privy Councillor von Wallot, architect of the Reichstag Building, Hohlwein was given the job of artistic director of the Dresden Landtag building. After savouring the rich flavour of this success he tried his hand at poster drawing as a side-line, and soon the side-line began to take precedence over everything else. One of his first poster designs was offered to Herm. Scherrer of Munich, and was accepted immediately. From then on Hohlwein turned out many thousands of poster creations for different publicity purposes, a number of which have been reproduced on postcards – and so, too, have the fine drawings of stags and chamois-bucks taken from *Ludwig Hohlwein's Jagdbuch*. Hunting was Hohlwein's one hobby.

Jessie Willcox Smith

This lovely Philadelphian lady was one of the United States' best-loved artists. Her work appeared on the covers of *Good Housekeeping*, inside the *Saturday Evening Post* and many of the women's magazines. Designs of Jessie Willcox Smith's 'children' bolstered the sales of a great variety of products, from Campbell's Soups and Ivory Soaps to Kodak Cameras. She adored children, despite remaining unmarried and childless herself, and her depictions of them always suggested magical combinations of eternal sunshine and flowers, and cool lush meadows – places where shadows never lurked to dim the smiling eyes of her children or halt their laughter. Unfortunately, there appears to be only one known set of postcards actually to have been signed by Jessie Willcox Smith. This set was published by Reinthal and Newman as series 100, but the titles of the six cards alone conjure up visions of the ideal happiness of children living in a world where the sun never sets. The titles of these splendid creations are ' 'The Lily Pool', 'Five o'clock Tea', 'In the Garden', 'The Green Door', 'Among the Poppies' and 'The Garden Wall'. But there must be other un-signed examples of Miss Smith's work on trade cards, as well as postcards.

Bert Thomas

Here is an artist who is fast becoming a favourite with postcard collectors. Born in Newport, Monmouth, Bert Thomas had the advantage of being the son of an artistic father, a sculptor by profession. In the early days of his career he created Cockney character cartoons for *Punch* and the *Evening News*. Then, early in the First World War, he drew a quick-fire sketch of a Cockney Tommy with a serene grin on his face, lighting his pipe in the face of an imaginary Kaiser. He donated it to the '*Weekly Dispatch* Tobacco Fund' for 'smokes' for the troops. This sketch was the famous, '' Arf a Mo', Kaiser' cartoon, described by the *Daily Mail* as 'the funniest picture of the War'. It also earned, via public subscriptions, donations, and the sale of its postcards, over a quarter of a million pounds. Bert Thomas continued to produce poster and postcard displays of his succinct satire right up to, and beyond, the Second World War, including many of Tommy Handley's 'ITMA' characters.

* * * * *

Very few of the names mentioned in these thumbnail biographies are very well known, but the postcard work of all these artists is avidly collected somewhere in the world. And, somewhere in the world, there can be found a huge variety of material relating to the lives and work of hundreds of other artists worthy of research. Old magazines dating from the turn of the century up to the mid-1930s are a wonderful source of information, and so are the libraries, museums and art galleries. All that is needed (apart from plenty of time and a lot of patience and determination) is the discovery of one meagre morsel of fact about the chosen subject, and the detection game has begun, bringing clue after exciting clue to be chased and analysed and the answers recorded. It is always a lucky bonus when the early days of research turn up the birthplace of the artist, for there is the place where there may be people who will remember their local celebrity, even living relatives and friends willing and only too anxious to reminisce with interested researchers. Every picture postcard which bears an artist's signature has a unique story to tell; look behind and beyond them and see the sketchbooks and easels.

1 A Red Cross Donkey of the
First World War.

2 Help for the Belgian soldiers.

3 First World War Food-Budget
series No. 386.

Copyright. **The late NURSE CAVELL.** Printed by permission.

BELGIAN SOLDIERS FUND
1916
OFFICIAL SOUVENIR

YOUR DRAWS
WILL NOW COST
YOU MORE !

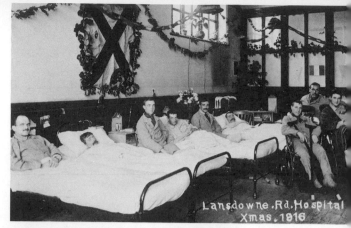

4 War casualties celebrating Christmas 1916.

Lansdowne. Rd. Hospital
Xmas. 1916

5 In praise of the nurses.

6 War or no war, windows still needed cleaning.

THE OCEAN ACCIDENT AND
GUARANTEE CORPORATION LTD
HEAD OFFICE 36-44 MOORGATE STREET.
LONDON
ASSETS EXCEED .250.0
CLAIMS PAID XCEE 500

*The lady window cleaners
of Nottingham.*

Titanic Firemen & Crew Memorial, Southampton Common. 1915.

7 Memorial to *Titanic* firemen and crew at Southampton, 1915.

8 HMS *Pincher* on active service.

ON ACTIVE SERVICE
THE
GREAT—1914—15—18—WAR

1914
ANTIVARA
DARDANELLES
1915
GALLIPOLI
GRAND LANDING
& MINE SWEEPING
KEREVES DERE
DUMEZ DERE
ANZAC

SUVLA BAY
DEDEAGATCH
1916
SKALA NUOVA
GULF OF SOLLUM
SALONICA

H.M.S. PINCHER

IN MEMORY OF OUR "CHUMMY" SHIP H.M.S. VANGUARD. FROM H.M.S. CONQUEROR.

TRAFALGAR DAY 1917

9 Trafalgar Day, 1917.

10 Captured
German
biplanes.

CAPTURED GERMAN BIPLANES. No 9.   COPYRIGHT

11 Army
airship
Delta, 1915.

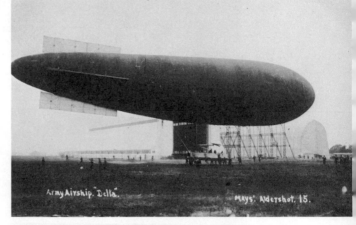

Army Airship. Delta.   Mays. Aldershot. 15.

12 British and
American
aviators on the
Western Front.

Aviadores británicos y americanos en el
frente occidental

13 General
Pershing at
Le Bourget.

GENERAL PERSHING VISITS THE AVIATION CAMP AT LE BOURGET.

14 Similar relief card showing a
French army balloon.

15 Advertising card for Jones
Sewing Machines, Leicester.

STATIONARY BALLOON. THE EYES OF THE ARMY.

A JONES SEWING MACHINE

RUNS AS SMOOTHLY AS AN
AIRSHIP

AND IS AS STRONG AS
A
DREADNOUGHT.

16 'On Active
Service' by
air, land and
sea.

BRITISH COMMISSARIAT WAGONS IN BELGIUM   *Active Service, No. 10*

17 A 'Farewell to Arms'
published by F. W. Woolworth
& Co.

18 One of the Union Jack Club
postcards.

The Union Jack Club, London.   *Copyright*

R. P. - 1058. La Guerre 1914-18 (Visé Paris 1958)
SOISSONS (Aisne) — L'Hôtel de Lorraine après les bombardements
Place de la Gare
Station and Place after the bombardment

19   L'Hôtel de Lorraine after bombardment.

20   A Belgian priest on his rounds.

3   Un prêtre Belge en équipement de guerre
A Belgian priest in war equipment

American Tank in Action

21   A British tank in American service.

22 Off-duty smiles.

23 On the way back to 'Blighty' at last.

THE START FOR "BLIGHTY"

Canadian Official

24 Peace at last for the Royal West Kents.

"Welcome Home to Royal West Kent's (1)"

25 The friendly 'corner shop' of the 1920s.

26 One of 'Ye Olde English Inns'.

27 The British Empire Exhibition at Wembley, 1924.

28 Food,
glorious
food – 24
hours a day at
Lyons.

29 A stand at the
Building
Exhibition,
Olympia,
1920.

30 All the fun of
the pageant at
Preston, 1922.

31 Major Segrave's 'Golden Arrow'.

32 Speed record-holder Major H. O. D. Segrave.

33 A faked American card.

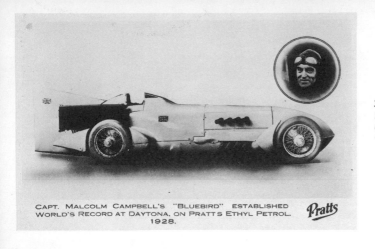

34 Captain Malcolm Campbell's 'Bluebird'.

CAPT. MALCOLM CAMPBELL'S "BLUEBIRD" ESTABLISHED WORLD'S RECORD AT DAYTONA, ON PRATTS ETHYL PETROL. 1928.

Pratts

35 Tennis champion William Tatem Tilden.

36 E. D. Mountain, athletics champion.

37 Captain C. A. Lewis at 2LO – early wireless station.

38 The Australian cricket team, 1926.

39 All aboard for a trip by charabanc.

His Master's Pride.

40 Alpha version of the famous HMV advertisement.

41 A beautiful lady and her lovely daughter.

MIRROR GRANGE.
SOUTH WEST VIEW.

42 The home of Pip, Squeak and Wilfred – Mirror Grange.

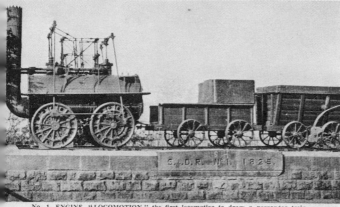

No. 1. ENGINE, "LOCOMOTION," the first locomotive to draw a passenger train,
STOCKTON & DARLINGTON RAILWAY. 1825.

43 No. 1 Engine, Stockton & Darlington Railway.

RAILWAY CENTENARY, 1925.
LOCOMOTION No. 1" hauling "original" train

44 Railway centenary of the No. 1 Engine, 1925.

Railway Station, Newbury

45 The Railway Station at Newbury.

47 James
Ramsay
Macdonald,
Prime
Minister
1924/1929.

J. RAMSEY MACDONALD

RED LETTER PHOTOCARD.

(Charles Chaplin.)   Charlie in Private Life.

46 The man who
made the
world laugh –
Charlie
Chaplin.

48 President
Wilson, US
President
1913–21.

PRESIDENT WILSON
The man who saved Europe.

49 'A Wee Scrap O' Paper is Britain's Bond' by Lawson Wood.

51 The victorious leaders of First World War Britain.

50 Tuck's Oilette series 3160 by Harry Payne.

52   One of the
G. Pipbot
patriotic postcards
'Vive la Belgique'.

53   Early 1914 French sketch by
Maurice Toussaint.

54   'Heroic Belgium', published by
C.W. Faulkner.

Cuirassiers - Tenue de route - 1914

Heroic Belgium.

'Wir müssen siegen und wir werden siegen!'

55 German patriotism.

56 One of the Swiss Bundesfeier cards.

57 Love conquers all — even from a tank!

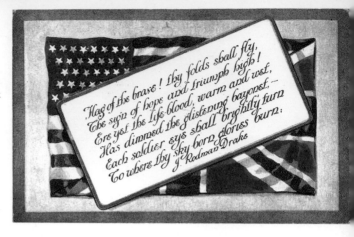

58 Old Glory
and Union Jack
join forces.

Flag of the brave! thy folds shall fly,
The sign of hope and triumph high!
Ere yet the life-blood, warm and wet,
Has dimmed the glistening bayonet,
Each soldier eye shall brightly turn
To where thy sky-born glories burn;
    J. Rodman Drake

59 Reassurance from spokesman
Fred Spurgin for Tommy.

60 Telling it to the Marines — an
age-old pastime.

DON'T YOU WORRY ABOUT US!

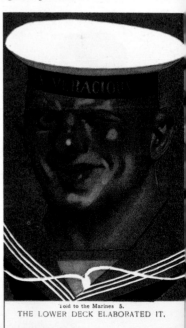

Told to the Marines 5.
THE LOWER DECK ELABORATED IT.

62 Greetings from a Japanese ally.

Greetings from one of your fair Allies.

ADVANCE AUSTRALIA!

'Sons of the Empire' ©   Copyright

61 'Sons of the Empire' — what
would we have done without them?

63 Ten feet tall!

When the Boys come Home.

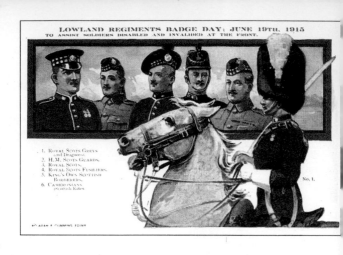

64 Relief card
for disabled
soldiers of
Lowland
Regiments.

65 Birn Brothers' tribute to the
Territorials.

66 And the Field Marshals.

67 A German
fund-raising
card.

68 Just like my Papa.

69 In praise of nurses.

NEW QUADRUPLE TURBINE · R.M.S. "LUSITANIA" · 32,500 TONS 68,000 HORSE POWER
LENGTH, 785 FT. BREADTH, 88 FT. DEPTH, 60 FT, 6 IN.

70 RMS *Lusitania*, sunk 7 May 1915.

'Britain Prepared'   By permission of H.M. Admiralty

FIRING FOUR 12-in. GUN SALVOES   [Reference No. 4

71 One of the 'Britain Prepared' cards from Photochrom.

72 'In the thick of it', in the 'Britain's Bulwarks' series.

73   Armoured motor
car (Tuck's 'At
the Front' Oilette).

74   A living
photograph from
the *Daily Mail*
battle postcards.

75   'Home' —
without the
comforts (a *Daily
Mail* battle card).

76 'It's the songs
ye sing and the
smiles ye wear.'

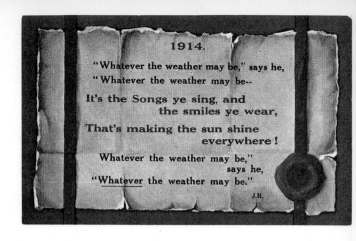

77 The Scouts' rally — 'Be
prepared . . .'

78 In 1917 the doughboys left
home for Europe.

IT'S A LONG, LONG WAY TO TIPPERARY (1).
Up to mighty London came an Irishman one day,
As the streets are paved with gold, sure ev'ry
one was gay;
Singing songs of Piccadilly, Strand and Leicester
Square,
Till Paddy got excited, then he shouted to them
there:—

79   'Goodbye Piccadilly.'

TAKE ME BACK TO DEAR OLD BLIGHTY. (2)
Take me back to dear old Blighty, put me on the train
for London town,
Take me over there, drop me anywhere,
Birmingham, Leeds, or Manchester—well, I don't care!
I should love to see my best girl, cuddling up again we
soon shall be;
Whoa! Tiddley-iddley-ighty, hurry me home to Blighty—
Blighty is the place for me.

81   Tommy's goal!

TILL THE BOYS COME HOME (3).
Over seas there came a pleading, "Help a nation in distress!"
And we gave our glorious laddies: honour bade us do no less;
For no gallant son of Britain to a foreign yoke shall bend,
And no Englishman is silent to the sacred call of friend.

80   'Through the dark clouds
shining.'

Gaze on it longingly,
Guard it with care.
You can't get another lump
Any old where!

82   A shortage of sugar, by Donald
McGill.

This isn't half a 'windy' place !

84   Another by McGill, published
by Inter-Art.

I've been collecting postmarks,
But when I look them through,
I can't find one among them all
That's come to me from you!

83   Donald McGill's plea for
postmarks.

86 The waiting game, by George
Studdy.

85 The two faces of Tommy —
on a mechanical postcard.

87 Old habits die hard, by
D. Tempest.

88 A sketch of
Tommy's life, by
F. Mackain.

Sketches
of Tommy's life
At the Base. — N° 4

" House " is the most popular game at the Base. Who hasn't heard those familiar lines : « Eyes down ! Legs eleven ! Kelly's eye Blind half hundred ! And another lucky old dip in the bag ! ».

89 A 'white
feather' type of
postcard.

90 Three men
and the 'last
match.'

THE LAST MATCH.

"ALL THE GIRLS WANT SOUVENIR BUTTONS
I WON'T PART WITH ANY MORE!"

91   Anyone got a safety-pin?

TOMMY COMES HOME ON LEAVE
TO-MORROW!

93   A Mabel Lucie Attwell pin-
up.

92   First World War German card
by P. O. Engelhardt.

Auf Vorposten!

95 The stars and stripes forever!

"*HURRAH*
FOR THE
STARS AND
STRIPES!"

94 Lovely American patriotic card
by René Barbier.

96 A French glamour card from
F. Fabiano.

97 French glamour by Maurice Pepin.

99 'La premiere leçon d'amour' by Leo Fontan.

98 'Ooh La la' in a shower, by Herouard.

100 Embroidered
silk postcard with
RFC crest.

101 Regimental embroidered silk
card with HLI crest.

102 Regimental embroidered crest.

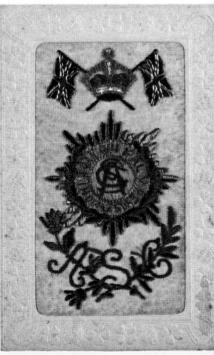

103 First World War embroidered birthday greeting.

105 A 'Home sweet home' embroidered birthday card.

104 Patriotic silk card, colourfully embroidered.

106 Embroidered envelope greeting card.

107 Silk-embroidered date card (envelope type).

108 British patriotic embroidered silk card.

BELAGERUNG.

109 Girl besieged by the German Army!

110 A patriotic card of St. Barbara.

St. Barbara, Schirmherrin der Kanoniere

Offizielle Karte für das rote Kreuz Kriegshilfsbüro, Kriegsfürsorgeamt.

111 Paddling back to peace.

MEERESBEUTE.

112 Japanese patriotic card — 'See all, hear all, say nothing!'

113 First World War French romance by Tito Saubidet.

TITO SAUBIDET. — Idylle en Alsace. — An idyll in Alsatia.

114 German wartime romance by Brynolf Wennerberg.

Fürs Vaterland!

La décoration finale.

THE FINAL DECORATION.

115   Peace at last! — or is it?

116   How about a game — of tennis?

117   'Wot yer got to laff at?'

Tennis.

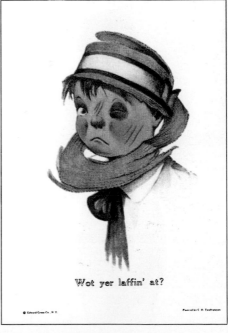

Wot yer laffin' at?

118 Lovely
Parisian card
evocative of the
twenties.

119 Fetching fashion from France.

120 A coy look from another
bathing belle.

122   Italian charm by Bianchi.

A PRAIRIE BELLE

121 American charm by Harrison
Fisher.

123   'Do not trust him, gentle
maiden!'

Nos bouches n'ont besoin que d'un baiser fervent
Pour exprimer l'émoi de nos cœurs confiants.

124 Speeding
into the twenties.

*Brooklands Favourites,
Mr Gordon Watney on 5°·6 Mercedes*

125 'The Girl and the Car' Oilette
series.

126 Another pair of 'girls' together.

127 Steaming
into the twenties
on a Tuck's
Oilette.

128 The 'Mauzan' charm.

129 Gorgeous nonchalance by
Herve.

No blinkin' light again—you never seem to keep them batteries topped up.

130 How the 'motor car' kept the kids happy.

131 And gardens were never the same again!

132 'Number please!'

ANOTHER TRADE KILLED BY MACHINERY!

HELLO! OLD THING! JUST WANT TO SAY I'LL BE PLEASED TO SEE YOU ANY DAY!

"When it comes to getting off the ground I can show the Greyhounds something!"

133 Trust Bonzo to get in on the greyhound act!

LAST WEEK I WAS HIT BY A BRICK— NOW—I'VE BEEN HIT BY THE SLUMP

135 An age-old story, Depression or not.

DON'T KNOW WHY MOTHER AND DAD GO TO TALKIES — THEY'VE NOTHING TO LEARN IN THAT RESPECT'

134 'To get away from you, Sonny Boy'?

136 A splendid example of an exhibition poster.

137 Another exhibition poster.

138 Colourful advertisement poster card.

139 Mechanical card to advertise a famous beer.

"WILLIAM YOUNGER'S FAMOUS BEER IS GOOD STUFF TO SELL FOR IT COMES UP NICE & CLEAR" AND/

140 'What am I supposed to be promoting?' asks Bonzo.

141 From the days when all children were good 'Ovaltinies'.

Das ist 'n Weg für meine Excelsior-Reifen!

BYE, BABY BUNTING
DADDY'S GONE A-HUNTING
TO BUY A TIN OF OVALTINE
TO FEED HIS LITTLE BABY ON
TO MAKE HER GROW UP BIG AND STRONG
BYE, BABY BUNTING

142 What a defence!

143 By Bert 'Arf a Mo' Thomas — and he's still at it!

144 What has he let himself in for?

WIRELESS TERMS ILLUSTRATED,
"A CRYSTAL RECEIVER."

145　And he's the 'cat's whiskers'!

"HASN'T FIDO LOVELY LIQUID EYES,
  AUNTIE?"
"YES, AND HE DON'T HALF WEEP!"

147　'Cheero' — another side to George Studdy.

All the best to you.

146　Do-it-yourself postal service.

148 Comedy
and a national
pastime.

149 A 'Felix the Cat' card.

150 Mickey Mouse in Germany.
©Walt Disney Productions.

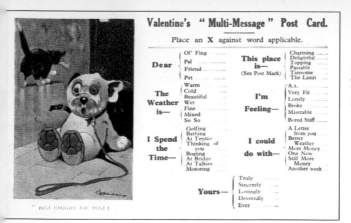

Valentine's "Multi-Message" Post Card.

Place an **X** against word applicable.

Dear	Ol' Fing / Pal / Friend / Pet	This place is— (See Post Mark)	Charming / Delightful / Topping / Passable / Tiresome / The Limit
The Weather is—	Warm / Cold / Beautiful / Wet / Fine / Mixed / So So	I'm Feeling—	A.I. / Very Fit / Lonely / Broke / Miserable / Bored Stiff
I Spend the Time—	Golfing / Bathing / At Tennis / Thinking of you / Boating / At Bridge / At Talkies / Motoring	I could do with—	A Letter from you / Better Weather / More Money / One Now / Still More Money / Another week
		Yours—	Truly / Sincerely / Lovingly / Devotedly / Ever

" JUST CAUGHT THE POST !

151 Just one example of the Valentine 'Multi-Message' cards.

152 'The Princess and the Pea', as seen by Kirchbach.

153 Aren't we all?

NIPPER SERIES

I'M EASILY TEMPTED

155 The young Bing Crosby.

154 The darling of early cinema,
Mary Pickford.

156 A good example of a deckle-
edged glossy greetings postcard.

157 Californian oranges for sale.

158 Where some of the money went in Alaska!

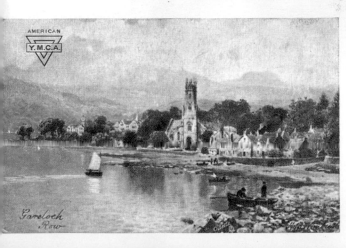

159 Tuck's Oilette, overprinted 'American Y.M.C.A.'.

160 Before smoking became an anti-social practice.

161 One of the Birn Brothers' Valentine cards.

162 A broderie anglaise greetings card.

163 Fine
American
advertising card.

164 Royal International Horse
Show card.

165 Happy 16th Birthday to a
Dutch princess.

166 Italian Art Deco.

167 One view of Art Deco fashion.

O SUSIE. IS YOU GOING FOR A BATHE OR
TO A FANCY DRESS BALL?

168 Art Deco from Mabel Lucie Attwell.

MABEL
LUCIE
ATTWELL

The Latest! What about it?

169 Anything
goes with loud
Art Deco
gingham checks.

170 Another Italian Art Deco
card.

171 Pure Art Deco by Joyce
Mercer.

172   Art Deco on the racecourse.

174   Art Deco in the garden.

173   Art Deco on ice.

176 Art Deco by Nashnyekov.

175 Early Art Deco fashion by
Mela Koehler.

177 Early Art Deco by
Montedoro.

179 Art Deco at Easter by Mela Koehler.

FROHE OSTERN

178 Art Deco in winter.

180 Precocious Art Deco by S. Bompard.

on va le voire

181 Brilliantly coloured romantic Art Deco.

183 Dutch Art Deco.

Gewitter.

182 Subdued Art Deco silhouette.

184 Attractive fairy-folk card.

185 Nursery Rhyme card from the twenties.

186 'In Pixie Land.'

187 Pip, Squeak
and Wilfred's
nursery in
'Mirror Grange'.

188 Into the jazz age with 'Jotter'.

189 When pyjamas became the
rage!

190 One of the cards from the 'Queen's Dolls' House' series.

191 Birthday card drawn by W. Barribal.

192 A card for Harvest Festivals of the twenties.

LOVING WISHES FOR YOUR BIRTHDAY

Your Birthday be filled,
With all kinds of delight ;
And happiest sunshine, -
From morning till night ! B2593

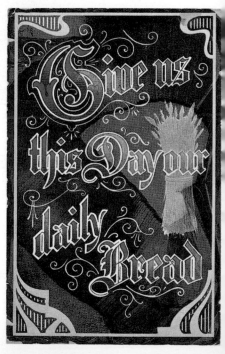

5 Notes on the Plates and Their Value

In the illustrated section of this book there is a good cross-section of collectable examples of postcards in black and white and in colour which were published between 1914 and 1930, and in the following plate descriptions not only has the rarity factor been included, but also the actual cost of each card at the time this collection was being assembled. These prices will almost certainly have fluctuated by the time this book is published, but at least they will give some substance to the asterisks used to indicate rarity. The key to rarity factors is as follows:

*	symbolizes the lowest valuation of plentiful postcards;
**	cards bordering on specialized categories;
***	specialized cards in limited supply;
**** R	demand well exceeds the supply;
RRR	almost impossible to find, and *very* expensive when they are found.

Plate 1 Photographic Red Cross relief card showing the progress of the 'Bosbury Red Cross Donkey', published by Tilley and Son, Ledbury. £2.50 ($5) ***

Plate 2 Relief card for the Belgian Soldiers Fund, 1916, published by Joseph Clarkson, Manchester. £2 ($4) ***

Plate 3 One of the First World War 'Food-Budget' series published by Art and Humour Co. £2.50 ($5) ***

Plate 4 Festivities at Christmas for war-wounded soldiers, anonymous publisher and photographer. £1 ($2) **

145

Plate 5 A lovely photographic card of nurses and their patients – anonymously produced. 75p ($1½) **

Plate 6 Keeping the home fires burning – and the windows shining. Women on war work card, published by C. & A. G. Lewis, Nottingham. £2 ($4) ***

Plate 7 Photographic card of the Titanic Firemen and Crew Memorial, Southampton, 1915, published by Rood Bros, Southampton. £1.50 ($3) ***

Plate 8 First World War Shipping card with lots of detailed information. Anonymous publisher and photographer. £2.50 ($5) ***

Plate 9 Unusual memory for 'Trafalgar Day', this photographic card of the wreath sent by the crew of HMS *Conquerer* to their former comrades of HMS *Vanguard* who died when their ship was blown up in July 1917. Anonymously published. £2 ($4) ***

Plate 10 A real photographic postcard of German biplanes in captivity, published in the St Andrew's Series. £5 ($10) ****R

Plate 11 Superb shot of the Army Airship *Delta* at her moorings. Published by May & Co., Military Photographers, Aldershot, 1915. £7.50 ($15) ***R

Plate 12 Spanish photographic card of aviators – anonymously produced. £5 ($10) ***

Plate 13 Relief card issued for the benefit of the National Federation of Discharged and Demobilized Sailors and Soldiers Fund. £4 ($8) ****R

Plate 14 Relief card issued for the same cause as the previous item, showing a close-up of an army balloon. £5 ($10) ****R

Plate 15 First World War advertizing sketch for the Leicester firm, A. Jones Sewing Machines – part of a set of some forty-odd cards which were privately published by the firm. £4 ($) ****R

Plate 16 Bright sepia tones with a bright orange border, published by Photochrom Co. Ltd, Tunbridge Wells, from the series 'On Active Service – by Air, Land and Sea'. £2 ($4) ***

Plate 17 Romance in silhouette type of card, published by F.

W. Woolworth & Co. Ltd during the First World War. 50p ($1)
**

Plate 18 Photograph of the Union Jack Club in London, published by the Club with a coloured colophon of the Union Jack on the reverse. £1 ($2) ***

Plate 19 One of the many postcards featuring war damage. Anonymous publisher. 50p ($1) *

Plate 20 Lovely photograph of a Belgian priest during the First World War, published by E. Le Deley of Paris, and distributed by William Ritchie and Sons Ltd, Edinburgh and London in the UK and British Colonies. £2 ($4) ***

Plate 21 This version of a tank in action was published by the *Chicago Daily News*, G. J. Kavanaugh War Postal Card Department. £7.50 ($15) ****R (In spite of the caption on the postcard the tank is British.)

Plate 22 One of the anonymously photographed and printed postcards showing soldiers off duty. £1 ($2) **

Plate 23 One from the *Daily Mirror* Canadian Official series. £1 ($2) **

Plate 24 An example of the many 'Welcome home' postcards, this one is from the Wells series, published by Harold H. Camburn, Tunbridge Wells. £2 ($4) ***

Plate 25 Peace time again, and a view of the friendly corner shop. Anonymously published. £5 ($10) ****R

Plate 26 And back to the friendly 'local' – in this case the Charlton Arms, Ludlow. Published by the Bristol Printing & Publishing Co. Ltd. £1 ($2) **

Plate 27 One of the many examples of postcard views of the British Empire Exhibition, Wembley. Published by the Concessionaires, Fleetway Press Ltd, Holborn. 50p ($1) * for unused mint cards; considerably more for those bearing the correct postmarks and stamps.

Plate 28 Fine example of nostalgic memories of Lyons' Corner Houses. Published by J. Lyons & Company Ltd. £5 ($10) ****R

Plate 29 One of the stands at the Building Exhibition held at Olympia in 1920. Published by Ernest Milner of Finchley. £2 ($4) ***

Plate 30 A good example of locally produced postcards, published by A. J. Evans of Preston. £1 ($2) **

Plate 31 A fine close-up of Major Segrave's *Golden Arrow*, published by Selfridge & Co. Ltd, London. £5 ($10) ****R

Plate 32 Complementary card to the previous illustration, showing a portrait of Major H. O. D. Segrave – also published by Selfridge. £4 ($8) ****R

Plate 33 A fake card using a backcloth, by Photo Station Studio, New York City. £1.50 ($3) ***

Plate 34 Very fine advert card for Pratts (Esso) Ethyl Petrol, with advertising blurb on the reverse. Published by Lilywhite Ltd. £10 ($20) ****R

Plate 35 Photograph of Wimbledon tennis player W. T. Tilden, three times World Champion, seven times American Champion. Published by E. Trim & Co. Wimbledon. £3 ($6) ****R

Plate 36 Real photographic postcard of E. D. Mountain, half-mile athletics champion at the England v. France games in 1922. Published by W. Berry, Rochdale. £1 ($2) ***

Plate 37 A lovely example of early broadcasting from station 2LO. Photograph by Archie Handford and printed in Croydon. £5 ($10) ****R̄

Plate 38 An official photograph of the Australian Cricket Team of 1926. Produced by T. Bolland, St Leonards-on-Sea. £2.50 ($5) ***

Plate 39 A photograph of one of the holiday charabancs, published by Perrochet-Mattie, Lausanne. £1.50 ($3) ***

Plate 40 An imitation of the imaginative advertisement for His Master's Voice records etc. Published by the Alpha Publishing Co. Ltd. £1.50 ($3) ***

Plate 41 One of the many photographs to feature Gladys Cooper – published by Rotary Photo, London. 50p ($1) *

Plate 42 'Mirror Grange', the house built for 'Pip, Squeak and Wilfred', the characters created by the *Daily Mirror*. Published by Raphael Tuck and Sons Ltd. (A coloured example of the interior of the nursery appears later on.) £1.50 ($3) ***

Plate 43 A card published in 1925 for the Centenary of the No. 1 Engine – published locally at Stockton. £3 ($6) ****R

148

Plate 44 Another card from the same publisher to show 'Loco-motion No. 1' being hauled again, one hundred years later. £5 ($10) ****R

Plate 45 The Railway Station, Newbury – published by J. T. Nash of Newbury. £4 ($8) ****R

Plate 46 One of the Red Letter Photocards showing Charlie Chaplin as himself – all these cards were published by Essanay with plain backs. £2.50 ($5) ***

Plate 47 Photograph of J. Ramsay MacDonald, the first Labour Prime Minister of Britain. Anonymously produced. £1.50 ($3) ***

Plate 48 A photograph of President Wilson, President of USA from 1913 to 1921. Anonymous publisher. £1.50 ($3) ***

Plate 49 A serious drawing by Lawson Wood from the 'St Clair' War series published by Dobson Molle & Co. Ltd of London and Edinburgh. This firm also published a similar series as cigarette cards for Thomson and Porteous, Cigarette Manufacturers of Edinburgh. This card is also on loan from Mr Paul Babb's collection. Value ***

Plate 50 This is one of the beautiful cards drawn by Harry Payne for Oilette series No. 3160 'Colonial Badges and their Wearers', published by Raphael Tuck and Sons during the First World War. £6 ($12) ****R

Plate 51 A pleasant montage of Britain's leaders during that war – published by B. & C., London, in the Savoy series. £3 ($6) ***

Plate 52 'Vive la Belgique' shows one of the hundreds of tinted bromide cards which were published by G. Pipbot of Paris during the First World War. £2 ($4) **

Plate 53 A colourful example of Maurice Toussaint's military cards – published in France. £5 ($10) ****R (in Britain and the United States but not in France)

Plate 54 A charming Belgian patriotic card, published by C. W. Faulkner, London. £1.50 ($3) ***

Plate 55 An appealing German patriotic card by R. von Wichera – 'We must conquer and we will conquer!' was a fine ambition for 1914, when this card was published in wartime Berlin. £3 ($6) ****R

Plate 56 One of the Red Cross Swiss Bundesfeier cards drawn by E. Burnand. £3.50 ($7) ****R

Plate 57 A lively cartoon-type patriotic card published in France. £2 ($4) **

Plate 58 Published by Gale & Polden Ltd, this card shows the union between the United States and Great Britain. £1.50 ($3) ***

Plate 59 This card comes from the 'Patriotic' series V11 published by the Inter-Art Co. London, showing Fred Spurgin at his perkiest. £1.50 ($3) ***

Plate 60 To have a set of these would brighten up any album! This card is No. 5 in the 'Told to the Marines' set, published by the Lawrence & Jellicoe series of postcards. The story goes:

1. The Admiral told a Story.
2. The Ward Room Approved it.
3. The Gun Room Adorned it.
4. The Petty Officers' Mess Expanded it.
5. The Lower Deck Elaborated it (illustrated).
6. The Marines Swallowed it.

And this is another card from the collection of Paul Babb. Value ***

Plate 61 'Advance Australia' is from the 'Sons of the Empire' series, published by the Photochrom Co. in their 'Celesque' range. £1.50 ($3) ***

Plate 62 Drawing pretty girls in their National costume, with patriotic overtones, was a favourite theme of many of the postcard artists during the First World War. This card shows one drawn by British artist W. Barribal – published by the Inter-Art Co. £2.50 ($5) ***

Plate 63 A cheerful type of patriotic card drawn by T. Gilson, published by E. J. Hey & Co., London. £1 ($2) **

Plate 64 This is card No. 1 of a set of six cards published by McLagan & Cumming of Edinburgh in aid of the Lowland Regiments Badge Day, 19 June 1915 to assist disabled soldiers. £5 ($10) ****R

Plates 65 and 66 Two cards published by Birn Brothers of London. The first is from series T and the second from series K; both are fine examples of British patriotism. The pair cost £4 ($8) ✱✱✱

Plate 67 An example of one of the German relief postcards issued during the First World War. £2.50 ($5)✱✱✱✱ R

Plate 68 One of the patriotic French postcards to be published by A. Noyer of Paris. £1 ($2) ✱✱

Plate 69 Originally published by Raphael Tuck and Sons, Ltd, this Nursing card is from a small collection of Oilettes which were reproduced by Mrs Sylvia Haynes in aid of the fund for the Elizabeth Garret Anderson Hospital. Value of original card £1 ($2) ✱✱

Plate 70 Published by Valentine and Sons, this view of RMS *Lusitania* was available a year before she was sunk on 7 May 1915. £2.50 ($5) ✱✱✱

Plate 71 Another card from publishers Photochrom of Tunbridge Wells. £1 ($2) ✱✱

Plate 72 Over-printed 'A happy Christmas', this card is from the Tuck's Oilette series No. 8739, 'Britain's Bulwarks – our Dreadnoughts'. £1 ($2) ✱✱✱

Plate 73 Another card from Raphael Tuck and Sons. This is one of Oilette series No. 8810, 'At the Front'. £2 ($4) ✱✱✱

Plates 74 and 75 Two of the coloured versions of postcards from the long series of the *Daily Mail* Battle Pictures. Plate 74 is card No. 4 from series 1, and Plate 75 is No. 20 from series 111. 75p each £($1.5) ✱✱✱ *Note*: the black and white cards in the series cost rather less.

Plate 76 A cheerful little song from 1914, published by E. Mack of London. 75p ($1.50) ✱✱

Plate 77 One of the popular Scouting cards, published by Valentine and Sons, Dundee. £2.50 ($5) ✱✱✱✱ R

Plate 78 A sentimental song-card No. 4953/1, published by Bamforth & Co. Ltd. 50p ($1) ✱

Plates 79, 80 and 81 These are three good examples of First World War 'pop' songs, with pictures which deserve a place in the social history section of postcard albums. All were published by Bamforth. 50p ($1) **

Plate 82 A card by the 'King of the Comic' card, Donald McGill, published by Inter-Art in their 'Comique' series No. 2393. £1.50 ($3) ***

Plate 83 McGill again, and the same publisher. This card is No. 2311 from the 'Comique' series. £1 ($2) **

Plate 84 And yet another from the same team – No. 1610 from the 'Comique' series. £1 ($2) **

Plate 85 One of the versions published by the Regent Publishing Co. Ltd, of Tommy Atkins wearing a mechanical hat. Turn the hat one way for smiles and the other for frowns. £2.50 ($5) ***

Plate 86 Superb example of First World War humour by 'Bonzo' artist, George Studdy – published by Valentine and Sons Ltd. £1.50 ($3) ***

Plate 87 Example of a comic war card by D. Tempest, published by Bamforth Ltd. 50p ($1) **

Plate 88 One of the 'Sketches of Tommy's Life' series by F. Mackain – published by G. Savigny of Paris, £1.50 ($3) ***

Plate 89 Hints to the un-uniformed were not always so polite! Anonymously published. £1 ($2) **

Plate 90 This card could be synonymous with the superstition that the third man to take a light from the same match was the target for the sniper's bullet. Published by the Woodland Card Company Ltd, London. £1.50 ($3) ***

Plate 91 An amusing card published by the Inter-Art Co. in their 'Terrier' series, No. 257. £1 ($2) **

Plate 92 Kriegspostkarte No. 77 by P. O. Engelhardt – with a 1916 Feldpoststation postmark on the reverse side. £5 ($10) ****R

Plate 93 One of Mabel Lucie Attwell's cherubs getting ready for Tommy to come home. Published by Valentine and Sons. £1 ($2) ***

Plate 94 United States patriotic glamour card by René Barbier. Anonymous publisher. £5 ($10) ***

Plate 95 Another American patriotic glamour sketch, published by the Philco Publishing Co. £3 ($6) ***

Plate 96 One of the French glamour cards by F. Fabiano from the series 'Les P'tites femmes', published in Paris. £4.50 ($9) ****R

Plate 97 An attractive example of French glamour cards by Maurice Pepin from the series 'Porte-Bonheur' – published in Paris. £5 ($10) ****R

Plate 98 Another lovely glamour card from Paris, entitled 'Une giboulée' by Herouard. £6 ($12) ****R

Plate 99 One of the coveted postcards by Leo Fontan, entitled 'La première leçon d'amour', published in Paris. £6 ($12) ****R

Plate 100 Embroidered silk card commemorating the Royal Flying Corps. Envelope-type pocket encloses another tiny greeting card. £10 ($20) ****R

Plate 101 Regimental embroidered silk card with vertical crest of the Highland Light Infantry. £12 ($24)****R

Plate 102 Regimental embroidered silk card with vertical crest for the Army Service Corps. £6 ($12)****R

Plate 103 Embroidered silk greetings card, published by Brodées 'La Pensée', Paris. £1.50 ($3)***

Plate 104 Embroidered silk patriotic card. £3 ($6)****R

Plate 105 Another Embroidered greetings card with an additional greetings sticker at the top. £2 ($4)***

Plate 106 An elaborately embroidered envelope-type card. £2.50 ($5) ***

Plate 107 Embroidered 'Date' card – envelope type. £3 ($6) ***

Plate 108 Horizontal embroidered patriotic silk card. £2 ($4) ***

Plate 109 Girl under 'siege' – published by Marcus Munk, Vienna. £3 ($6)***

Plate 110 A card of St Barbara, Patron Saint of German Artillerymen. Published in Vienna. £4 ($8) ****R

Plate 111 An exhilarating paddle in the bay at the end of the First World War – published by Marcus Munk, Vienna. £3 ($6) ***

Plate 112 A Japanese patriotic postcard – published in Japan. £1.50 ($3) ***

Plate 113 First World War romantic card, 'An idyll in Alsatia' by Tito Saubidet. Published by P. J. Gallais et Cie, Paris. £5 ($10) ****R

Plate 114 An example of Brynolf Wennerberg's work – published in Berlin by Dr Eysler & Company. £5 ($10) ****R

Plate 115 'La décoration finale' – and baby makes three! Sketched by Sherie and published by the Inter-Art Co. £1 ($2) ***

Plate 116 'Anyone for tennis? Not today, thank you.' could be the caption to this card by T. Gilson – published by E. J. Hey & Co. London. £1 ($2) ***

Plate 117 There was nothing much to laugh at by the time the war ended, and this card by C. H. Twelvetrees, published by Alpha, seems an appropriate choice for stepping into the unknown twenties. £2 ($4) ***

Plate 118 This pretty girl wears one of the new cloche hats with a detachable wide brim. A lavishly tinted card, published by E. K. & Co. Paris. £1 ($2) **

Plate 119 Tinted card revealing the new open-laced sides of bathing suits – published by P.C. of Paris. £2.50 ($5) ***

Plate 120 Another tinted bathing beauty card, published by A. Noyer of Paris. £2.50 ($5) ***

Plate 121 One of a long line of pretty American girls painted by Harrison Fisher and published by Reinthal and Newman, New York. £2 ($4) ***

Plate 122 An example of Italian post-war fashion and beauty by Bianchi – published in Milan. £3 ($6) ***

Plate 123 Tinted romantic card, published by R.T.B. of Brussels. £1 ($2) **

Plate 124 One of the 'Brooklands Favourites' cards published by Valentine and Sons Ltd. £8 ($16) ****R

Plate 125 An early 1920s card published by Raphael Tuck and Sons Ltd, from Oilette series No. 3034, 'The Girl and the Car'. £2 ($4) ***

Plate 126 A French tinted version of the girl and car theme. £2 ($4) ***

Plate 127 Steaming into the twenties – one of the lovely Tuck's Oilettes from the 'Famous Expresses' series No. 3547. £2 ($4) ***

Plate 128 Italian elegance drawn by Mauzan and published in Milan. £6 ($12) ****R

Plate 129 'La Cigarette' by G. Hervé – published in Paris. £8 ($16) ****R

Plate 130 Many of the artist-drawn cards which feature children have a great nostalgia value – like this one by Vera Paterson. Anonymous publisher. £1 ($2) **

Plate 131 And this one published by Bamforth, from the 'Tempest Kiddy' series No. 431, drawn by D. Tempest. It bemoans the passing of horse-drawn transport! £1 ($2) **

Plate 132 The automatic telephone had not yet reached the children drawn by Nora Annie Birch, and published in the Beaux Arts Reliable series. 50p ($1) **

Plate 133 George Studdy's 'Bonzo' getting in on the new craze for greyhound racing. Published by Inter-Art in the 'Comique' series No. 3816. £1.50 ($3) ***

Plate 134 Another by D. Tempest from Bamforth & Co. 'Tempest Kiddy' series, this time to pin-point the advent of the 'Talkies'. £1 ($2) **

Plate 135 An alphabet card by Mabel Lucie Attwell which draws attention to the American slump in 1929. Published by Valentine and Sons Ltd. £1 ($2) **

Plate 136 This superb poster-type card was issued to mark the *Internationale Postwertzeichen Ausstellung*, in Vienna 1923. The designs for the postcard and the Exhibition stamps on the reverse side were drawn by Ludwig Hesshaimer – and this card also carries the right postmark. £20 ($40) RRR

Plate 137 Another poster-type Exhibition card – published by Robert Lang of Paris. £8 ($16) ****R

Plate 138 A colourful French poster advertising card, drawn by A. Farcy and published in Marseilles. £5 ($10) ****R

Plate 139 Although this is **not a postcard**, but a double sided mechanical advertising card for Younger's Beer, it is an example of one of the related items of ephemera collected by postcard enthusiasts. On the illustrated side the beer is being drawn; turn the card over and, presto, the beer is being drunk! £15 ($30) RRR

Plate 140 A rare advertising card for Excelsior-Reifen motor tyres – published by the manufacturers. £25 ($50) RRR

Plate 141 An attractive advertisement postcard by Phyllis Cooper for Ovaltine. £5 ($10) ****R

Plate 142 One of the popular 'Are you a Mason' cards, published by Millar and Lang in their National series. £3 ($6) ***

Plate 143 A fine example to show the humour of Bert Thomas of – "Arf a Mo, Kaiser' fame – published by Raphael Tuck and Sons. £3 ($6) ***

Plate 144 And the humour of Lawson Wood – published by Inter-Art. £1.50 ($3) ***

Plate 145 A nice twist to the advent of broadcasting by I. MacBean – published by the Photochrom Co. Tunbridge Wells. £1 ($2) ***

Plate 146 This card by G. F. Christie was also published by the Photochrom Co. £1.50 ($3) ***

Plate 147 Fido bears a passing resemblance to Bonzo in this postcard – not surprising, since the signature 'Cheero' was the pseudonym used occasionally by George Studdy. Published by Humoresque. £1 ($2) **

Plate 148 Illustrating the craze for crossword puzzles which started in the 1920s, this card was published in the National series by Millar and Lang. £3 ($6) ****R

Plate 149 Advertising 'Felix the Film Cat' which appears exclusively in Pathé's *Eve and Everybody's Film Review* – published by Inter-Art. £4 ($8) ****R

Plate 150 A German example of Walt Disney's creation Mickey Mouse. £6 ($12) ****R

Plate 151 Illustrating a double craze – Bonzo and Valentine's 'Multi-Message' postcards. £2.50 ($5) ***

Plate 152 One of a series of Dutch cards illustrating fairy tales by Kirchbach – forerunners to a spate of 'Snow-white and the Seven Dwarfs' cards. £1 ($2) ***

Plate 153 A card from the 'Nipper' series by Brian White – published by Valentine and Sons Ltd. £1 ($2) **

Plate 154 Mary Pickford, the beautiful American actress and film star. Published by J. Beagles. £1.50 ($3) ***

Plate 155 This postcard portraying a young Bing Crosby was published by DE RESZKE Cigarettes. £3 ($6) ***

Plate 156 Glossy greetings cards similar to this one were all the rage in the twenties period. Anonymously published. 25p ($50c) *

Plate 157 An American card with a linen finish – published by the Western Publishing and Novelty Co. Los Angeles, California. £1 ($2) ***

Plate 158 Another colourful American card, linen finished and published by Curteich, Chicago. £1 ($2) **

Plate 159 A Tuck's Oilette from series No. 7508 'Gareloch' by H. B. Wimbush. Overprinted American Y.M.C.A. £1 ($2) **

Plate 160 An unusual greetings card, published by Birn Brothers of London and New York. £2 ($4) ***

Plate 161 Embossed Valentine card, also published by Birn Brothers. £3 ($6) ***

Plate 162 Embroidered greetings card produced by Raphael Tuck and Sons for the 'Broderie D'Art' series. £5 ($10) ****R

Plate 163 A fine American advertising card to publicize the Wallace Memorial Edition of *Ben-Hur* published by Sears, Roebuck and Co. Chicago. £5 ($10) ****R

Plate 164 Publicity postcard for the International Horse Show held at Olympia, London. £2 ($4) ***

Plate 165 A Dutch postcard to commemorate Queen Juliana's sixteenth birthday in 1925. £2.50 ($5) ***

Plate 166 Italian card of Art Deco design, 1925. £2.50 ($5) ***

Plate 167 The zig-zag striped slacks topped with polka-dots put this card by Freda Mabel Rose into the Art Deco category. £1 ($2) ***

Plate 168 An Art deco card by Mabel Lucie Attwell, published by Valentine and Sons. £2 ($4) ***

Plate 169 Art Deco ginghams boldly displayed by Chloe Preston. Published by Valentine. £2 ($4) ***

Plate 170 Another Art Deco design from Italy. £2.50 ($5) ***

Plate 171 One of Joyce Mercer's splendid Art Deco cards – published by C. W. Faulkner. £5 ($10) ****R

Plate 172 A clever Art Deco card by Maggy Moñier – published in France. £8 ($16) ****R

Plate 173 A charming Art Deco sketch by Chiostri – published by Ballerini & Fratini, Florence. £6 ($12) ****R

Plate 174 One of the lovely Art Deco designs drawn by C. Shand – anonymously published. £6 ($12) ****R

Plate 175 Art Deco at its best by Mela Koehler. Published in Germany. £15 ($30) RRR

Plate 176 A gorgeous Art Deco example by Nashnyekov – published in Italy. £10 ($20) ****R

Plate 177 A fantastic Art Deco design by M. Montedoro – again published in Italy. £15 ($30) RRR

Plate 178 Art Deco in winter – published in Italy. £2 ($4) ***

Plate 179 An Art Deco Easter card by Mela Koehler – published in Germany. £15 ($30) ****R

Plate 180 Art Deco by S. Bompard – published in Belgium. £2.50 ($5) ***

Plate 181 Sailing up the river in Art Deco style – in bright Clarice Cliff colour. Published in Italy. £3 ($6) ***

Plate 182 An unsigned Art Deco silhouette, 'Stormy Weather', published in Germany. *Note:* some desirable Art Deco silhouette cards are drawn by artists Marte Graf amd Manni Grosze. £3 ($6) ***

Plate 183 An attractive Art Deco example from Holland. £2.50 ($5) ***

Plate 184 One of Molly Brett's charming 'fairy-folk' cards – published by C. W. Faulkner. £2.50 ($5) ***

Plate 185 A Nursery Rhyme card by Flora White, published by J. Salmon. £2 ($4) ***

Plate 186 'In Pixie Land' published by A. M. Davis. £2 ($4) ***

Plate 187 The nursery, 'Mirror Grange' – Pip, Squeak and

Wilfred's House – built by the *Daily Mirror*. Published by Raphael Tuck and Sons Ltd. £2 ($4) ***

Plate 188 Everybody's doing it!' Shades of the Jazz age by 'Jotter' – published by Woolstone Bros in their Milton series. £2 ($4) ***

Plate 189 The 'Pyjama Game' as seen by Mauzan – published in Italy. £6 ($12) ****R

Plate 190 'The King's Bedroom' from The Queen's Dolls' House series Three, Oilette No. 4502 – published by Raphael Tuck and Sons Ltd. £3 ($6) ***

Plate 191 An attractive birthday greeting by W. Barribal – published by the Inter-Art Co., Barnes, London. £3 ($6) ***

Plate 192 An attractive illuminated postcard published in Germany. On the reverse of this is written: 'And in visiting Temples I had forgotten that You are everywhere, even on a postcard.' £3 ($6) ***

6 Where to Buy and Sell Early Postcards

The market-place for buying and selling old postcards is no different from any other where items of specialized interest are concerned. Since the 1960s, when the present-day craze for collecting postcards was revived, enough cards have passed through the hands of established dealers for them to recognize at a glance the difference between the rare and the common – and for the examples which they know to be rare they will always pay a good price.

The difficulty comes when they are offered collections 'which must be very valuable because so-and-so said they were in the *Daily Shout* (or whatever) last week.' Publicity of this kind is usually followed by dealers being offered bundles and boxes and albums of the type of cards they do not want and cannot sell at any price. Only very occasionally does an 'eye-popping' collection come the way of a dealer as a result of articles appearing in the Press.

So how can the non-postcard-collecting sections of the public assess the value of unwanted cards which they either already possess or may expect to acquire in the future? There are catalogues which evaluate postcards that they could buy, but they would have to know something about cards to understand them. They could perhaps visit postcard fairs and come away flushed with excitement at the sight of some of the prices marked up on cards which appeared to be very similar to their own, or they could study the illustrations in postcard books like this one. But whatever method vendors choose to assess the value of their collections they must also keep in mind the difference between buying and selling before offering collections to a dealer.

When buying stock, dealers are on the constant lookout for the popular quick-selling categories of postcards, and for these they will usually pay up to half catalogue price for cards marked under one pound, and up to three-quarters of the selling price for the more expensive variety. They are not interested in buying large assortments of common views of churches, castles, civic buildings, and glossy greetings cards – unless there is a fair balance of more exciting postcards included to help justify the cost. And they are definitely not interested in cards which are creased, cracked, too dirty to be cleaned, or have their corners missing!

Assuming that all the homework has been done, and a reasonable collection of cards in fair condition has been assembled, the next step is to find an interested buyer – and for this purpose this list of many dealers who buy and sell cards has been compiled.

Shops and other venues for personal callers

Branch Two (John Jeeves), 36 Queen's Road, Brighton, Sussex. Tel. 0273 24827

Bath Stamp and Coin Shop, 12/13 Pulteney Bridge, Bath, Avon. Tel. 0225 63073

Crest Collectors Centre, Allington, Maidstone, Kent. Tel. 0622 52011

Dendelti (Bob and Betty Roberts), 44 Vale Street, Upper Gornal, Dudley, West Midlands, DY3 3XF. Tel. 09073 4372

Ducal (Jack and Thelma Duke), 228a Shirley Road, Southampton, Hants SO3 1HR. Tel. 0703 38766

David Field Ltd, 42 Berkeley Street, Mayfair, London W1X 5FP. Tel. 01 499 5252

Francis Field, Richmond Road, Sutton Coldfield, West Midlands. (Aviation only.)

J. A. L. Franks Ltd., 140 Fetter Lane, London EC4A 1B5. Tel. 01 405 0274

J.A.L. Franks Ltd, 22 Bond Street, Brighton, Sussex. Tel. 0273 686120

Stanley Gibbons Ltd, 391 Strand, London WC2R 0LX. Tel. 01 836 8444

John Hall and David MacWilliams, 17 Harrington Road, South Kensington, London SW7. Tel. 01 584 1307

Hendon Collectors' Centre (Clive Smith), 1 Newark Parade, Greyhound Hill, London NW4. Tel. 01 203 1772

Alex Jackson, 81 Station Parade, Harrogate HG1 1ST. Tel. 0423 55430

Lake and Brooks Ltd, 106 Bedford Chambers, Covent Garden, London WC2E 8HH. Tel. 01 836 6370

Garnet Langton, Burlington Arcade, Bournemouth, Dorset. Tel. 0202 22352

David A. Lee & Co. Ltd, 11 Tombland, Norwich, Norfolk. Tel. 0603 613227/0603 712675

Leeds Card Centre, 41–43 New Briggate, Leeds LS1 6NU. Tel. 0532 468404

Faith Legg, Waveney Bookshop, 13 Castle Street, Eye, Suffolk. Tel. 037987 308

Leicester Philatelic Auctions Ltd. (Retail Dept.), Northampton Square, Leicester LE1 1PH. Tel. 0533 537034

London Postcard Centre, 21 Kensington Park Rd., London W11. Tel. 01 229 1888 (Saturdays only)

David and Rosemary Matthews, Burton Collectors' Centre, 24 Derby Street, Burton-on-Trent, Staffordshire. Tel. 0283 48494

Murray Cards International (Martin Murray), 76 Barnet Way, Mill Hill, London NW7 3AN

Past Delights (Peter Bullen), 1 Chapel Street, Guildford, Surrey. Tel. 0483 39595

Pleasures of Past Times (David Drummond), 11 Cecil Court, Charing Cross Road, London, WC2 4NEZ. Tel. 01 836 1142

Recollections (Michael and Angela Steyn), 2 Monkville Parade, Finchley Road, Temple Fortune, London NW 11. Tel. 01 458 1026

The Stamp Shop (Ray and Christine Shapland), 13 Cross Street, Barnstaple, N. Devon BX31 1BD. Tel. 0271 5581

The Stamp Shop (C. H. Spink), 34 St Nicholas Cliff, Scarborough YO11 2ES. Tel. 0723 65221

Transy News (Editor: Harold Richardson), Shop address: 27b Marchmont Road, Edinburgh EH9 1HY. Tel. 031229 8043

Vale (Bill Varnham), 21 Tranquil Vale, Blackheath, London SE3 0BU. Tel. 01 852 9817

Winchester Stamp Centre, 6 Parchment Street, Winchester, Hants. Tel. 0962 62491

Dealers who publish sales lists

Golden Age Postcards (Tony Byatt), 28 St Peter's Road, Malvern, Worcestershire WR14 1QS.

Ron Griffiths. 47 Long Arrotts, Hemel Hempstead, Hertfordshire HP1 3EX. Tel. 0442 59019

Brian and Mary Lund, 27 Walton Drive, Keyworth, Nottinghamshire. Tel. 06077 4087

Gordon and Honor Webb, 53 Twinbrook Park, Swanpool, Falmouth, Cornwall.

George Wolstenholme, 13 Westroyd Park, Mirfield West Yorkshire. Tel. 0924 493471

Dealers who join most of those listed above at Postcard Fairs

Jane Nicholson, 8 Aspen Walk, Stourport, Worcestershire. Tel. 02993 4839

Presland Postcards, P.O. Box 38, Basingstoke, Hants. Tel. 0256 781744

Scene Before (Eric McKercher), P.O. Box 23, Bedford, MK41 8BR.

Shelron (Ron and Shellah Grosvenor), 18 New Road, Abbey Wood, London SE2. Tel. 01 310 3399

Solent City Postcards (Doug and Dory Whitfield), 33 Meadow-bank Road, Fareham, Hants.

Solent Enterprises (Ron and Carol Emmott), 2 Fourways, Church Hill, West End, Southampton SO3 3AU. Tel. 04218 4862

Brian Swallow, Great Western Antique Centre, Bartlett Street, Bath, Avon.

Organizers of Postcard Fairs

IPM Promotions, (J. H. D. Smith), Kingscote Station, East Grinstead, Sussex. Tel. 0342 21796 (Monthly Fairs held at the Bloomsbury Centre Hotel, London WC1 and Central Hall, Westminster, London SW1.)

RF Postcards, 17 Hilary Crescent, Rayleigh, Essex. Tel. 0268 743222 (Monthly fairs at the Eccleston Hotel, London, SW1, and other venues.)

Shelron (Ron and Shellah Grosvenor), 18 New Road, Abbey Wood, London SE2. Tel. 01 310 3399 (Monthly fairs at London, Cardiff and Birmingham.)

Coin, Stamp & Postcard Fairs (Mark Jarmain), P.O. Box 9 York. Tel. 0904 32331 (Weekend events, countrywide, throughout the year.)

Auctioneers who hold regular sales of postcards

Sotheby's Belgravia, 19 Motcomb Street, London SW1X 8LB. Tel. 01 235 4311

Phillips, 7 Blenheim Street, New Bond Street, London. Tel. 01 629 6602

Christies, 85 Old Brompton Road, London SE7. Tel. 01 581 2231

MCC/SPA (Ken Lawson), 24 Watford Road, Wembley, Middlesex. Tel. 01 908 2636 (Monthly Auctions of postcards at Caxton Hall.)

West London Auctions, Sandringham Mews, High Street, Ealing, London W5. Tel. 01 567 6215

Lake and Brooks Ltd, Postcard Auctions, 106 Bedford Chambers, Covent Garden, London WC2E 8HH. Tel. 01 836 6334 (Auctions held at the Eccleston Hotel in conjunction with the RF Postcard Fairs.)

United Kingdom Postcard Clubs

Postcard Club of Great Britain, Mrs Drene Brennan, 34 Harper House, St James' Crescent, London SW9.

Avon Postcard Club, Mrs Marion Freeman, 24 Cherry Orchard, Pershore, Worcestershire.

Huddersfield and District Postcard Society, George Wolstenholme, 13 Westroyd Park, Mirfield, Yorkshire.

Leeds Postcard Club, Mrs A Whitelock, 9 Brentwood Grove, Leeds LS12 2DB.

Lincoln Collectors' Club, T. G. Collier, 2 Wickenby Close, Fosse Estate, North Hykeham, Lincolnshire.

Norfolk Postcard Club, P. J. Standley, 63 Folly Road, Wymondham, Norfolk.

Bradford and District Postcard Club, A. E. Wood, 26 Front View, Shelf, Halifax, West Yorkshire.

Tees Valley Collectors' Club, A. J. Lambert, 15 Glenfield Road, Darlington, Co. Durham.

London Postcard Club, Mrs J. Cohen, 58 Sandringham Road, London, NW11.

North of England Postcard Club, F. A. Fletcher, 35 St Georges Terrace, East Bolden, Tyne and Wear.

Study Circle for Early Numbered Tuck Postcards, Mr Tony Warr, Fairview, Ickford Road, Shabbington, Aylesbury, Buckinghamshire.

Kent Postcard Club, Jack Smith, Pattison Farm, Aldington, Kent.

Northern Ireland Postcard Club, Roy Campbell, 70 The Green, Dunmurry, Co. Antrim, Northern Ireland.

The Suffolk Postcard Club, Mrs Peggy Southgate, 8 The Green, Mistley, Manningtree, Essex.

Newcastle upon Tyne Postcard Club, Mrs M. Osborne, 26 Balmoral Terrace, South Gosforth, Newcastle upon Tyne.

Rushden, Northants Postcard Club, Mr B. C. Church, 2 Meadow Drive, Highham Ferrers, Rushden, Northants.

Maidstone Postcard Club, Mrs I. Hales, 40 Hildenborough Crescent, Maidstone, Kent.

Sussex Postcard Club, Mr Dave Bull, 12 The Broadway, Lancing, Sussex.

Hertfordshire Post Club, Neil Jenkins, 113 Bramble Road, Hatfield, Hertfordshire.

Canal Card Collectors Circle, Mr A. K. Robinson, 56 Henley Avenue, Dewsbury, W. Yorkshire.

Surrey Postcard Club, Simon Burke, 7 Sandfield Terrace, Guildford, Surrey.

United States of America Postcard Clubs

Metropolitan Postcard Collectors Club, New York City, Rose Shiffrin, 16–18 212th Street, Bayside, NY 11360.

Lone Star Postcard Collectors Club Texas, Floy Case, 2300 Lincoln, Fort North, TX 76106.

Great South Bay Postcard Club, Long Island, NY, Dorothy Miller, 29 Wilson Drive, Babylon, NY 11704.

Bay State Postcard Club, Boston, MA, Mrs Anne Miller, Box 344, Lexington, MA 02173

Rhode Island Postcard Club, Mr Robert J. Andrews, P.O. Box 361, Pawtucket, RI 02862.

Central New York Postcard Club, Ruth R. Weimer, RD 2-Box 173, Route 31, Canastota, NY 13032.

Webfooter Postcard Club, Oregon, Evelyn Greenstreet, 7426 S/W 31st Avenue, Portland, OR 97217.

Windy City Postcard Club, Chicago, The Secretary, WCPCC, Box 8118, Chicago, Illinois, 60680.

Capitol Beltway Postcard Club, C. R. Collins, 19 Empire Place, Greenbelt, MD 20770.

Houston Postcard Club, Texas, Mrs Kathryn Parker, 10803 Hunters Forest, Houston, TX 77024.

The Upstate Postcard Club, Schenectady, Gayle Balmuth, Box 101, Amsterdam, NY 12010.

Morlattan Postcard Club, PA, Mrs Kenneth Kirk, 16 Rosedale Drive, Pottstown, PA 19464.

The Postcard Club, PA, Marie Lord, 4613 Eugene Drive, Bristol, PA 18977.

Maple City Postcard Collectors Club, Elkhart, Indiana, Miss Alice Reed, 65449 CR3, Route 1, Wakarusa, IN 46573.

Golden Gate Postcard Club, Florence Ogden, P.O. Box 412, San Francisco, CA 94101.

Wolverine Postcard Club, Laura N. Goldberg, 1313 E. Harry, Hazel Park, MI 48030.

Equine Deltiologists of America, Debbie Curtiss, Route 2, Box 314, Yakima, WA 98902.

Western New York Postcard Club, Mrs Nancy Williams, 3520 Atlantic Avenue, Penfield, NY 14526.

Twin City Postcard Club, Minn., Teri Weinandt, 2717 Colorado Avenue, South, St Louis Parl, MN 55416.

Cuba International Postcard Club, New York, Frank J. Pichardo, P.O. Box 1116, Flushing, NY 11354.

Duneland Postcard Club, Gary, Indiana, Charlotte North, 2633 Stevenson, Gary, Ind. 46406.

Wichita City Postcard Club, Chicago, Hal Ottaway, Box 18282, Wichita, KANS 67218.

Chrome Card Collectors Club, New Jersey, The Secretary, Box 508, Bound Brook, NY 08805.

Garden State Postcard Collectors Club, NY, Mrs Helen Briel, 506 William Street, Scotch Plains, NJ 07076.

Indianapolis Postcard Club, Indiana, Edith Brown, 3908 N. Graham, Indianapolis, IND 46226.

Washington Crossing Card Collectors Club, PA, The Secretary, P.O. Box 39, Washington Crossing, PA 18977.

Monumental Postcard Club of Maryland. Baltimore, Mrs Peggy Bower, 2902 Ontario Avenue, Baltimore, MD 21234.

Gateway Postcard Club, Pat Villmer, 2741 Edwin, St Louis, MO 63122.

Western Reserve Postcard Society, Cleveland, Betty Toth, 13538 Shady Oak Boulevard, Cleveland, Ohio 44125.

Sunshine Postcard Club, Florida, Dorothy Laughlin, 711 S/W 73rd Avenue, Miami, Florida 33144.

Postcard Collectors Club of Buffalo, NY, Mrs J. R. Wheatley, 294 Claremont Avenue, Buffalo, NY 14223.

Heart of Ohio Postcard Club, Betty Neiner, Colony Apartments, 1085-D Merimar Circle, Columbus, Ohio 43220.

Postward Pals, Local Iowa Club, Mrs Thomas Weiland, 5362 Northwood Court, Route 5, Dubuque, IA 52001.

South Jersey Postcard Club, Gloria Downes, 100 Champlain Avenue, Wilmington, DE 19804.

Expo Collectors & Historians Organization, Edward J. Orth, 1436 Killarney Avenue, Los Angeles, CA 90065.

Richmond Postcard Club, John Whiting, Antique Village, 6700 Chamberlayne Road, Mechanicsville, VA 23111.

Some AMERICAN sources of postcards

Rita and Harry Nadler, P.O. Box 4318, Thousand Oaks, California.

Mrs Sally Carver, 179 South Street, Chestnut Hill, Mass.

Peter Polous, *Little Red Caboose*, P.O. Box, 1085, Irving, Texas.

Roy and Marilyn Nuhn, P.O. Box, 562, West Haven, Connecticut.

Commemoratives International Ltd, Jonah R. Shapiro, 1027 University Building, Syracuse, New York 13202.

Some FRENCH sources

Edouard Pécourt, 58 bis, rue du Louvre, Paris.

Kiki Werth, 28 rue Bubillot, Paris 7501.

Patrice Boubet, Passage dechambre, 33 rue Falguière 75015 Paris.

BELGIUM

Tim Johnston, 42 Ave Capitaine Piret, Brussels.

Some GERMAN sources of postcards

Mike Clarke, *Desiderata*, Postfach 5362, D78 Freiburg, West Germany.

Willi Bernhard, 2000 Hamburg, 73 Wiesenredder 2, West Germany.

Some postcard priced CATALOGUES

IPM Catalogue of Picture Postcards, published by J. H. D. Smith.

Picton's Priced Postcard Catalogue and Handbook, by Maurice R. Hewlett, published by B.P.H. Publications, Chippenham, Wiltshire.

L'Argus International des Cartes Postale, published by Gérard et Joelle Neudin, Paris, France.

Catalogue des Cartes Postale Anciennes, by Andre Fildier, Paris, France.

Postcard periodicals published in the United Kingdom

Postcard Mail – monthly tabloid newspaper. Subscription £4 per annum. Editors: Maurice Bray and Colin Rhodes-Doughty, BRD (Publishing) Ltd, P.O. Box 39, Loughborough, Leicestershire.

Reflections of a Bygone Age – bi-monthly magazine. Subscription £2.00 per six issues. Editors: Brian and Mary Lund, 27 Walton Drive, Keyworth, Nottinghamshire.

Transy News – bi-monthly magazine. Subscription £1.75 per annum. Editor: Harold Richardson, 27b Marchmont Road, Edinburgh EH9 1HY.

Postcard World – bi–monthly magazine – subscription £2.50 per annum. Editor: Mrs Drene Brennan, 34 Harper House, St James Crescent, London SW9.

Postcard Collectors' Gazette – monthly magazine. Subscription £7 per annum. Managed by: David Pearlman, 36 Asmuns Hill, London NW11.

Newsletter – bi–monthly Avon Club news and views. Subscription £2 per annum. Editor: Mrs Marion Freeman, 24 Cherry Orchard, Pershore, Worcestershire.

Hertfordshire Postcard Magazine – published three times a year. 45p per copy. Editor: Ron Griffiths, 47 Long Arrotts, Hemel Hempstead, HP1 3EX, Hertfordshire.

Postcard Traders Association

The annual British International Postcard Exhibition (BIPEX) held at Central Hall, Westminster, London SW1, is organized by the Postcard Traders Association. Hon. Secretary: 17 Hilary Crescent, Rayleigh, Essex. Tel. 0268 743222

Bibliography

The following books are recommended for further reading.

American Guide to Tuck's, Sally Carver, Carver Cards, U.S.A., 1977.

Book of Bathing Beauties, Ronnie Barker, Hodder and Stoughton, U.K., 1974.

Book of Boudoir Beauties, Ronnie Barker, Hodder and Stoughton, U.K., 1976.

British Exhibitions and their Postcards, F. A. Fletcher and A. D. Brooks, U.K., 1978.

Cartes Postales Art Nouveau, Alan Weill, Paris, France, 1977.

Collecting Silk Postcards, C. Radley, Barking, U.K., 1976.

Discovering Picture Postcards, C. W. Hill, Shire Publications, U.K., 1970.

Edwardian Entertainments – A Picture Postcard View, C. W. Hill, M. A. B. Publishing, U.K., 1978.

Erotic Postcards, Barbara Jones and William Ouellette, Macdonald and Jane's, U.K., 1977.

Fantasy Postcards, William Ouellette and Barbara Jones, U.S.A., 1975.

French Undressing, Paul Hammond, Jupiter Books, U.K., 1976.

History of Silk Postcards, C. Radley, Barking, U.K., 1975.

Illustrators of Postcards from the Nursery, Dawn and Peter Cope, East West Publications, U.K., 1978.

L'Aeronautique a la Belle Époque, George Naudet, Belgium, 1976.

Louis Wain: The Man who Drew Cats, R. Dale, William Kimber, U.K., 1970.

Picture Postcards, Marian Klamkin, David & Charles, U.K., 1974.

Picture Postcards and their Publishers, Anthony Byatt, Golden Age Postcard Books, U.K., 1978.

Picture Postcards and Travel, Frank Staff, Lutterworth Press, U.K., 1979.

Pictures in the Post, Richard Carline, Gordon Fraser, U.K., 1971.

Picture Postcards in the United States 1893–1918, George and Dorothy Miller, U.S.A., 1976.

Picture Postcards of the Golden Age, Toni and Valmai Holt, Mac-Gibbon and Kee, U.K., 1971 (reprinted 1978).

Postcards for Pleasure – Series One, Tom Browne, Series 2, Lance Thackeray, compiled by Ken Lawson and Tony Warr, U.K., 1978/1979.

Sauce!, Ronnie Barker, Hodder and Stoughton, U.K., 1978.

Stevengraphs, Geoffrey Godden, Barrie & Jenkins, U.K., 1971.

The Comic Postcard in English Life, F. Alderson, David & Charles, U.K., 1969.

The Embroidered Silk Postcard, C. Radley, Barking, U.K., 1977.

The England of A. R. Quinton, J. Salmon, Salmon, U.K., 1978.

The Picture Postcard and its Origins, Frank Staff, Lutterworth Press, U.K., 1966 (reprinted 1979).

The World of Donald McGill, M. Tickner and B. Buckland, U.K., 1974.

The Woven Silk Postcard, C. Radley, Barking, U.K., 1978.

Till the Boys Come Home, Toni and Valmai Holt, MacGibbon and Kee, U.K., 1977.

With Love – *The Erotic Postcard*, Erik Norgaard, MacGibbon and Kee, U.K., 1969.

Index

173